The Sorcerer's Tale

FAITH AND FRAUD IN TUDOR ENGLAND

ALEC RYRIE

OXFORD
UNIVERSITY PRESS

OXFORD

UNIVERSITY PRESS

Great Clarendon Street, Oxford OX2 6DP

Oxford University Press is a department of the University of Oxford.
It furthers the University's objective of excellence in research, scholarship,
and education by publishing worldwide in

Oxford New York

Auckland Cape Town Dar es Salaam Hong Kong Karachi
Kuala Lumpur Madrid Melbourne Mexico City Nairobi
New Delhi Shanghai Taipei Toronto

With offices in

Argentina Austria Brazil Chile Czech Republic France Greece
Guatemala Hungary Italy Japan Poland Portugal Singapore
South Korea Switzerland Thailand Turkey Ukraine Vietnam

Oxford is a registered trade mark of Oxford University Press
in the UK and in certain other countries

Published in the United States
by Oxford University Press Inc., New York

© Alec Ryrie 2008

British Library Cataloguing in Publication Data

Data available

Library of Congress Cataloging in Publication Data

Ryrie, Alec.
The sorcerer's tale: faith and fraud in Tudor England / Alec Ryrie.
p. cm.
ISBN 978-0-19-922996-3
1. Wisdom, Gregory, d. 1599. 2. Swindlers and swindling–England–History–16th century.
3. Magic–England–History–16th century. 4. Westmorland, Henry Neville, Earl of,
1524 or 5–1564. 5. Conspiracies–England–History–16th century.
6. Crime–England–London–History–16th century. 7. England–Social conditions–16th century.
8. Great Britain–History–Tudors, 1485–1603. I. Title.
HV6692.W57R97 2008
364.16'3092–dc22   2008024477

Typeset by SPI Publisher Services, Pondicherry, India
Printed in Great Britain
on acid-free paper by
Clays Ltd, St. Ives plc

ISBN 978-0-19-922996-3

1 3 5 7 9 10 8 6 4 2

For Ben

Contents

List of Illustrations

Chronology

1541 November	Gregory Wisdom is sued over a shipment of fine fabrics
1541–2	John and Gregory Wisdom are sued for unlicensed medical practise
1542 June	John and Gregory Wisdom are given a royal licence to practice medicine
1543 November/ December	Gregory Wisdom in the household of Sir Nicholas Wentworth
1544 January	Wentworth's servants visit Gregory Wisdom's house in London
1544 November	Gregory Wisdom meets Henry, Lord Neville, in London
	Lawsuit between Gregory Wisdom and Sir Nicholas Wentworth is heard
1544 December	Gregory Wisdom and Ninian Menville leave for the North of England
1545 March	Wisdom and Lord Henry meet for the last time
1546 September	Lord Henry is arrested
1547 January	Death of King Henry VIII: accession of Edward VI
March	Lord Henry is pardoned
1549	John Wisdom leads a consortium leasing Painters' Hall from the Painter-Stainers' Company
	Lord Henry becomes the fifth earl of Westmorland

1553 February	John Wisdom's application to join the Royal College of Physicians is rejected
May	Gregory Wisdom is imprisoned for 'words touching the King's Majesty's person'
July	Death of King Edward VI: accession of Mary I
1558	Death of Queen Mary I: accession of Elizabeth I
1559	John Wisdom makes his will
1562	Death of John Wisdom
1564	Death of Henry Neville, fifth earl of Westmorland
1570	Gregory Wisdom in dispute with Hector Nuñez of the Royal College of Physicians
1582	Gregory Wisdom is admitted to the Royal College of Physicians
1599	Death of Gregory Wisdom

Foreword

Like the subject of this book, I find myself leading a double life. I have a day job as a church historian at one of Britain's more traditional universities; I am even a lay preacher in the Church of England. But this project has led me down some pretty seamy byways. I have spent more time than I should have done immersing myself in subjects like gambling, fraud, necromancy, astrology, prostitution, and syphilis. Along the way I have read some very peculiar things and had some very unusual conversations (a few frankly alarming ones) with some very intriguing people. And what might have been a worthy, steady piece of academic history has turned into something more sensational. I feel that I owe myself, and you, an explanation.

The respectable reason for writing this book is that it opens up a slice of history rarely seen. The story which I am telling here lifts the carpet on some murky aspects of English life in the sixteenth century—organized crime, black magic, gambling, and prostitution—and reveals some connections between them and the more salubrious worlds of court, nobility, university, and Church. Its moral, if a story like this can have a moral, is that (as always) the gates separating the rapacious from the respectable were easily climbed. And it tells us something about how the great ideological ferments of the Tudor age—religion, politics, philosophy—were connected to one another and also to more basic concerns and more animal appetites.

But for me, too, the respectable version is only part of the story. The truth is that in 1998, when I was in the Bodleian Library in Oxford researching for my PhD, I stumbled across a summary of Henry, Lord Neville's confession (the document now at the heart of Chapter 1). I was enthralled by the story, fractured and incomplete as it was; but it had nothing to do with my research and I had to leave it to one side. Still, it stuck in my mind like a burr, and in 2000 I returned to it without quite knowing why. A little bit of digging produced a hint as to the mysterious central character's real identity, and from there on I was hooked. For seven years I have been working on and off on the subject, squeezing in a few hours' research here or there into the cracks between more pressing or more po-faced projects. Each time I thought the trail had gone cold, a chance conversation or a glance at an index threw up some fresh leads. I kept at it, and ultimately wrote the book, because it has been fun. I think Gregory Wisdom's story is a story that deserves to be told; I hope you will agree.

I first had a stab at writing about this material as a party piece for an academic conference. But as more material surfaced, and more connections emerged, my lectures on the subject became longer, more involved, and darker. Numerous audiences, from sixth-formers to academics, have helped me to thrash out some of the problems. The members of the Shakespeare Institute in Stratford stick in my mind as the most challenging and encouraging. It eventually became clear that a book-length treatment was the only way to do justice to the material, although I have tried to keep the book as short as possible. Even now, most of Wisdom's secrets remain hidden.

What follows is not a full-scale biography: not nearly enough evidence about Gregory Wisdom's life survives for that. It is more like a damaged portrait, of the kind so common in the Renaissance. Although the image of the central figure is obscured in places, we can see the context in which he stands, and that context can help us decipher the portrait's riddles. So as well as telling Wisdom's own story—fragmentary as it is—the book delves into the worlds in which he moved: medical, aristocratic, religious, magical, criminal. Looking at Wisdom through each of these lenses allows us to piece together more of what his story means. At the same time, his exploits help to illuminate subjects which are themselves mysterious.

Researching Wisdom's career has taken me far beyond the historical fields I know best, and I have depended heavily on borrowed expertise—generously given, as always amongst academics. Innumerable people have fielded odd queries relating to different aspects of this project. Some helped to stop me dashing up blind alleys; others opened up new possibilities. Those who come to mind are Keith Dockray, Bruce Janacek, Lauren Kassell, Frank Klaassen, Robert Mathieson, Peter Maxwell-Stuart, Sophie Page, Margaret Pelling, Catherine Richardson, Mike Riordan, and Matthew Woodcock; my apologies to those I have forgotten. I am also grateful to the ever-helpful staff at the National Archives, the British Library, the Folger Shakespeare Library, the Royal College of Physicians, and the Guildhall Library. Particular kudos goes to Elaine Fulton, Deborah Jewison, Peter Marshall, and (not least) my parents, each of whom read the whole text in draft and made invaluable comments. Oxford University Press's anonymous readers encouraged the project while also gently pointing out several embarrassing errors. Matthew Cotton shepherded the book through the Press apparently effortlessly; Luciana O'Flaherty, the commissioning editor at OUP, was forthright in her advice and kept badgering me when I needed it.

Numerous friends and colleagues have become heartily sick of my regaling them with the latest exploits of 'my sorcerer', but have hidden it well. (Now that the book is out, I promise I will stop.) Above all, each time I have come home triumphantly with some new twist of the evidence, Victoria has met it with renewed belief. But the book's dedication goes to Ben, who isn't yet old enough to read stories, let alone stories as murky as this one. I hope that when the time comes he will enjoy it.

1

The Nobleman

THE case seemed like a juicy but straightforward scandal. All the ingredients were there: aristocracy, lust, envy, attempted murder, and the mighty brought suddenly low. In September 1546, Henry, Lord Neville, the eldest son and heir of the earl of Westmorland, was accused of conspiring to murder his wife and his father. The nature of the proposed murders was more sensational still. Lord Henry, it was claimed, was relying not on the nobility's traditional methods (poison, anonymous ruffians in the street) but on malevolent magic. King Henry VIII's principal secretary, Sir William Paget, called it an 'unnatural and inhuman enterprise' and took personal charge of the investigation. The young nobleman was thrown into London's Fleet Prison, a rare celebrity in such a dank and fetid place. From there, he wrote a series of desperate letters to Paget, pleading to be spared the penalty which his alleged crimes carried: death by hanging as a common felon.

In truth, however, Lord Henry was less the villain of the crime than its victim. This book is about the real villain: a shadowy, slippery figure whose silver tongue and sharp practices led to Lord Henry's imprisonment. This man's name was Wisdom, and he led a double, or triple, life as a respectable physician; as a practitioner of forbidden magical arts; and as a con-man, trickster, and a part of London's criminal fraternity. Wisdom would not have wanted his own story to be told, and he did not make it easy for us to do so. We must piece it together from scattered and incomplete sources, and even then all we have is a series of fragments, not the full picture.

But there are compensations. As we follow this evasive man's footprints through the archives, he will act as a guide to the seamy underworld of Tudor England, a world often intimately connected to the more respectable England of court, nobility, and university. On the journey, we will find out a good deal about crime, magic, disease, sex, and religion in the sixteenth century, and about the connections between them. These contexts help us to make some sense of Wisdom's story. Through them, Wisdom's story will help us to make some sense of Tudor England, a world less distant from our own than we might like to think. The world he will show us is precarious, turbulent, and ravenous; a country where a man could make, or take, fortunes—if, like Wisdom, he was ruthless and quick-witted enough to grasp the opportunities.

The trail starts with Wisdom's most illustrious victim: Henry, Lord Neville, the hapless would-be murderer. From his prison, on 18 November 1546, Lord Henry dictated a detailed confession to a secretary. It ran to eight large, closely written pages, and in it he gave an abject account of his supposed crime and of how he had been led into it. It is through this account that we first meet Wisdom. And so it is with Henry, Lord Neville that we must begin.

If a confidence-trickster, of the sixteenth century or any other, were to design his ideal victim, he would bring together a range of traits. Wealth, obviously. But the target must not only have money, but also be needy, or greedy, for more. He should not be too bright, or too clever a talker, but instead be easily befuddled or dazzled. And of course, he should not be entirely honest. No one can be swindled quite so effectively as someone who can be tangled in the webs of his own deceits and guilty secrets.

Henry, Lord Neville fitted this profile perfectly. His lineage and the title that he was heir to were grand, and carried wealth enough; but they were faded, dingy glories, relics of a past when the titled nobility had been England's backbone. The Nevilles were one of the oldest families in England, and their power in their County Durham heartland was still formidable. But they had never really recovered from the division of the family's lands in the 1420s, and under the Tudors, the political winds were set against them and their kind. A century or two earlier, English kings had readily delegated authority over the North to the Nevilles and their like; but the Tudors preferred administrators like Cardinal Wolsey and Thomas Cromwell, low-born men who rose by their own ruthlessness and who were not independently powerful. The old nobility were still disorientated by the discovery that they were no longer in control.

Lord Henry's father, Ralph, the fourth earl of Westmorland, had an unspectacular political career. He sat on Henry VIII's Council for a few months in 1526, and was not invited back. Worse, the family was tainted with treason. Earl Ralph's childhood guardian, the duke of Buckingham, was executed for real or imaginary plots against Henry VIII in 1521; and in the autumn of 1536, the whole family was caught up in a vast peasant rebellion that swept the North of England, a rising commonly known as the Pilgrimage of Grace. It was a dangerous time for Northern magnates, as they tried to decide whether to oppose the wave of anger at Henry VIII's tyranny, or to ride it. Unheroically, but sensibly, Earl Ralph did both. He gave some signs of support for the rebels, and some of them certainly believed that the Nevilles could be relied upon to back their cause. Indeed, the head of a cadet branch of the family actively supported the rebellion, although he later claimed that he had only done so under duress. Once the rebels had been tricked into disbanding and their leaders rounded up, Earl Ralph, too, managed to persuade the King that his actions were blameless and, indeed, that he had placed himself in considerable danger. In the end, the crisis cost the Nevilles nothing more than a little public humiliation, and it could have been much worse. Nevertheless, it did nothing to halt the family's slow drift into political irrelevance.

It is in 1536, the year of the Pilgrimage of Grace, that we first have sight of Ralph's son, young Lord Henry. He was 12 years old, and the rebellion was a terrifying experience for him. Earl Ralph was briefly taken captive by the rebels early on. In order to secure his own release, he offered his son to the rebellious armies as a hostage. This craven gesture was cloaked in splendour. The young Lord Henry came to the rebels bearing the banner of St Cuthbert, the Anglo-Saxon saint whose shrine at Durham was one of the North's great pilgrimage centres, and with whose cult the Nevilles had long been associated. It was a powerful symbol of the old order which the rebels claimed to be defending: a Catholic North headed by the traditional nobility. But Lord Henry was no more than an honoured prisoner whose fate was dependent on the rebels' good opinion of his family. In the end, he was released unharmed, but this wrenching episode must have marked him. It certainly represents the first appearance of what would become a pattern in his life: Lord Henry was a man to whom things happened, not one who made things happen. The experience may not have endeared the old religion to him. Nor would it have made him love his father. Less than a decade later Lord Henry was plotting the old man's murder.

His other intended victim was also already on the scene in 1536. In July of that year, a few months before the rebellion, Lord Henry had married Lady Anne Manners, the daughter of the earl of Rutland. On the same day, one of Lord Henry's sisters married Lady Anne's brother and the other, the earl of Oxford's son. The triple wedding was a memorable society event, and the reception at the earl of Rutland's London home was graced (briefly) by the King's own presence; but the spectacle masked the fact that none of the three families thus united had political influence to match the grandeur of their titles. Lord Henry would not have been surprised to be married off while still a boy, although a bare 12 was a little young even for a blue-blooded bridegroom. Dynastic marriages were the sinews of the aristocracy. Lord Henry and his new wife were expected to put on a show of conjugal affection and to set about continuing the Neville family line. That much, at least, they did. By 1543 Lady Anne had had two sons, and perhaps one or more daughters (whose arrival was less interesting). It was honestly, or half-honestly, expected that in these circumstances couples would learn to love one another. But for young Lord Henry, it seems marriage was simply another kind of polite captivity.

Nevertheless, as his family expected, he set about applying himself to politics. He began to be found at the royal court. When Henry VIII's fourth wife, Anne of Cleves, was welcomed from Germany in January 1540, Lord Henry was a face in the crowd. At some point in the following four years, he acquired a minor office at court, as a carver in the

King's Privy Chamber—a ceremonial sinecure, fitting for a young nobleman. If he was making a reputation, though, it was as a soldier. He deputized for his father in organizing the defence of the Scottish Border in 1541, and rallied to the Border again during an invasion scare in 1543. And in August 1544, he took part in the massive assault on the city of Boulogne which Henry VIII directed in person. When the city fell to the English the following month, the King knighted him in recognition of his services. It was a proud moment, although not as great an honour as it looked: Henry VIII was so delighted by the victory (his first of any substance for thirty years, and, as it turned out, an empty one) that he handed out knighthoods with abandon. Lord Henry's career was not (yet) disgraceful, but nor was it distinguished.

It was his conduct away from the battlefield which would have recommended him to a fraudster looking for a fool who could be parted from his money. In London, Lord Henry was drawn into city ways. London's underworld hooked its claws into the young man. By the end of 1544, he had developed a serious gambling habit, and the inevitable debts which went with it—for as we shall see, London's gambling houses were not so simple as to let their customers win. Lord Henry's father, Earl Ralph, disapproved of the gambling, or at least of the debt, and relations between father and son became further strained. Worse, Lord Henry's relationship with his wife, Lady Anne, was icy. Why we do not know, but what is clear is that the gambling houses provided Lord Henry with an easy solution to this particular problem, for many of them doubled up as brothels. He was, it seems, a regular customer of both.

This, then, was Henry Neville at the age of 20: blue blood, unremarkable career, unhappy marriage, mounting gambling debts, and not a great deal of sense. For the criminal underworld which was already profiting from his follies, he was a lucrative prospect.

Here we can pick up Lord Henry's own account of events. On the whole, it seems trustworthy; he was abjectly confessing his faults rather than trying to gloss over them, and he certainly emerges from the story with very little credit, although he may have massaged the truth in a few specific places. The story begins one morning in November 1544, not long after Lord Henry's return from Boulogne. His father was on the family estates in the North of England, and so Lord Henry himself was, for the time being, head of the Neville household in London. On the morning in question, he was walking in the garden at the family house, and was approached by a man named Ninian Menville.

Menville is one of the more unpleasant characters in this story. He was a decade or more older than Lord Henry, and was a Scot by birth and by name. It is likely that he was a Borderer from the West Marches of Scotland, for he was particularly familiar with the Maxwell family who dominated those parts. As his career makes plain, he was at home with the brutality of Border ways; and as his service to an English lord suggests, he was also at home with treachery. He was now a Neville family retainer, and a particular favourite of Lord Henry's mother, Countess Katherine. Her favour had saved his life seven years earlier, in 1537, when Menville had been facing the noose for committing a violent robbery. Countess Katherine had successfully begged for a royal pardon. Menville had continued to serve the family, as well as serving as a soldier on the Scottish Border in 1543. By 1544, he had insinuated himself into young Lord Henry's confidences. And it was on this morning that he delivered the young man to the wolves.

As Lord Henry recalled, Menville approached him in the garden and said,

> My lord, I know that you are far in debt, and know not which way to pay the same; also you have lost much money by play, and daily do.

It was, no doubt, an open secret in the Neville household that the young master was gambling, and falling deeper into debt. But Menville had a suggestion.

> But yet, if you will follow my counsel, I can devise such a way for you whereby you may both recover your loss and also win as much as shall pay your debts, and have enough to serve yourself besides from time to time.

Who would not want to hear more? The chance to 'serve himself' would have been particularly appealing—Menville, it seems, knew about the prostitutes as well as the gambling. Lord Henry asked him to elaborate. Menville then said that 'there were men that could, by art, make a ring that, whosoever had the same upon his finger, should win all that he played for'. If the dice were falling against him, magic could be used to tilt the table.

Lord Henry was intrigued. In his defence, it should be said that the idea was not so preposterous as it seems to us. He knew that dice-play was not an honest business, and that professional gamblers hid their secrets like gold. He knew, too, that magical and quasi-magical secrets were taken seriously by some of the most brilliant minds of his age. And of course secrecy itself has a wicked allure. The jaws of the trap—a little wealth, and an unscrupulous desire for a little more—locked shut, eased by gullibility. The victim had been snared. Lord Henry asked to know more.

Now began the slow and careful game of drawing him in. The main gambit was to throw seeming obstacles in his path, so that he would become more determined, more desperate, and more deeply implicated. Menville explained that he did not know of any such magicians, but added that he thought one of the servants of the household might. Lord Henry immediately summoned this servant, a man named George Stafford, and explained the idea. Stafford admitted that indeed he did know of someone with the necessary skills, but he professed to be very reluctant to get involved. Any such magical practice was, he pointed out, against the law. It was an important point. Two and a half years earlier, in 1542, Parliament had passed England's first-ever statute against magic. This is commonly referred to by historians as the Witchcraft Act, but it encompassed far more than witchcraft, and was properly titled the Act against Conjurations, Witchcrafts, Sorcery, and Enchantments. It prescribed death by hanging for magicians who performed any of a wide range of magical acts, and also—critically—for their accomplices. Stafford warned that the magician he knew might be unwilling to take the risk, and that by approaching him they might be endangering themselves. It was the 1542 Act under which Lord Henry was eventually arrested, and from the first it was an important part of the snare in which he was caught. Under the Act's draconian terms, as soon as he consulted a magician, he had already committed a capital offence. It was a threat which could be, and was, used to buy his silence.

Stafford's caution may have given Lord Henry pause, for Menville quickly intervened with a more optimistic view:

> What danger can it be...to any man as long as it is not known? And if it may be brought to pass we shall be all made by the same, and able to recompense the worker.

The price was being made explicit to Lord Henry: a con-spiracy of silence from which there would be no easy escape. Later, when the secret was out and he was facing the hang-man, he lamented that he had succumbed at this point to Menville's 'crafty persuasions', but he was also honest enough to blame his own 'earnest desire'. Stafford agreed to find the magician.

The next step was carefully stage-managed. Early the fol-lowing morning, while Lord Henry was still in bed, Menville burst into his chamber to announce the news: Stafford had not only found the man but had actually brought him to the house. Lord Henry hurriedly dressed while Menville described the newcomer. He was impressed by him: he 'seemeth to be both wise and wealthy', Menville claimed, and drew particular attention to his sharply dressed appearance. He was not, Lord Henry learned, 'in a threadbare coat as commonly these unperfect multipliers be'. *Multiplier* was a derogatory term for sham alchemists, those who claimed to be able to multiply precious metals. Menville warned that Stafford's magician was a cut or two above such street-corner wizards, and was 'well apparelled like a cunning man in his craft'. This was a professional, an expert, whose skill com-manded respect and whose dignity was in keeping with Lord Henry's status. Indeed, Menville urged his master to hurry, 'for such rich men love not to give long attendance'. Lord Henry was already being thrown off balance and put at a dis-advantage. For what it is worth, however, Menville's warnings were partly true. From the moment this magician appears on the scene, it is apparent that he was a class act. Quite apart from his fondness for fine and exotic clothing—which will become familiar—he was a charismatic, resourceful, and polished operator for whom poor Lord Henry was no match. Lord Henry scrambled hastily out of bed, and as soon as he was dressed, received the visitor, a man to whom he referred throughout by a single name: Wisdom.

Lord Henry, flustered, tried to take control of the interview. He began by saying that he had heard of Wisdom's skill in astronomy, through which he might be able to make a ring which would give Lord Henry better luck with the dice. This talk of astronomy was, perhaps, a polite evasion. Astronomical or astrological magic was, as we shall see, the most respectable form of magic in the sixteenth century. Importantly, it was not banned under the 1542 Act. Wisdom smoothly cut across his client, explaining that he could indeed make the ring he wanted, but that he would not be using any such innocuous means. Instead, he would do so by conjuring spirits, whom he would command to perform magical services for him. This was a capital offence. Wisdom added that there were two ways that he might make such a ring: 'both by a good spirit and an evil'. Having held up this alarming pair of choices, he added reassuringly, 'But I will work it for you by the holy angels, because it shall be of the more virtue.' Nothing but the best for the old nobility. Of course, he added, this was the more expensive of the two options.

They now began to negotiate terms. There was, again, a show of reluctance. Wisdom insisted that he made his living legitimately, as a physician, and that he did not undertake such extracurricular activities lightly. He performed magic, he said, only for his 'dear friends', and he proceeded to explain quite how dear. He emphasized that the ring would be worth a fortune to Lord Henry—two or three thousand pounds before Christmas, he guessed airily. As such, he would make it only if Lord Henry would guarantee him a pension of £20 a year for life.

Wisdom must have known that this was an impossible request. It was a huge sum: enough for a man to retire on comfortably. But while he could not hope to get such an enormous amount of money, he could use the request to set the parameters of the negotiation, and this is what happened. Lord Henry's counter-offer was itself very high, no doubt higher than anything he had been expecting to give, for he simply halved Wisdom's bid to offer a pension of £10 a year. However, he also added two conditions. First, the pension would only be paid if the ring worked. Second, the payments would begin when Earl Ralph died and Lord Henry inherited the title and the incomes that went with it; a clause which suggests how much his inheritance was on Lord Henry's mind, and which may have sowed the seeds of a later plot. In the meantime, Wisdom would have to make do simply with a share of the winnings which his ring secured.

Wisdom accepted this offer: the deal was done, and now the game proper could begin. He told Lord Henry that work on the ring would begin the following day, only now hinting at how long the work was likely to take. He also told him that he would need some money up front 'to buy all such things as were necessary': he asked for four marks, a *mark* being two-thirds of a pound. Expenses had not been part of the deal, but Lord Henry could only pay up.

It was in fact three days before Wisdom returned to begin the project, but when he did arrive, he did so in earnest. He had decided to move into the Neville household for the duration. For the next month he availed himself of the best old-fashioned aristocratic hospitality. Lord Henry had not expected the fabrication of a ring, however magical, to take quite so long. He was further concerned that Wisdom did not actually appear to be doing any work on the project, but rather was going out and pursuing his own business every day. But when he worked up the courage to challenge Wisdom, he found that the magician had an answer to everything.

Wisdom explained that he was working on the ring as fast as he could, but that he could only do it for two hours out of every twenty-four—between 3 and 4 a.m., and between 5 and 6 p.m. This was not because he was dragging his feet, but because the work was being done by angels, and such a workforce had particular requirements that need to be accommodated. If Wisdom was moonlighting from his day job as a physician, the angels, too, were having to fit in their ring-making tasks around their daily obligations of singing praise to God. 'Therefore,' he explained, 'they must be taken, before their matins and after their evensong.' Lord Henry unhappily accepted this explanation and waited.

Wisdom's next move was, again, perfectly timed. On Christmas morning, he came into Lord Henry's bedchamber and wakened him—another sign of how far he had insinuated himself into the household. He had a Christmas present for his employer: the ring was finished. Wisdom showed it to him, but did not give it to him. Instead, he gave him a contract, which he required Lord Henry to sign and seal on the spot. The contract committed Lord Henry to the £10 annuity he had promised, but as he sat up in bed and read it, he was alarmed to discover that it specified that the annuity should start immediately, not from the date of the old earl's death as they had agreed. Wisdom made light of this. He said that he had no intention of holding Lord Henry to those terms, and that the clause was put there simply so that the annuity would be paid if Lord Henry should predecease his father. Amazingly, Lord Henry accepted this, signed, and finally got his hands on the precious ring. Now was his chance to reverse his fortunes.

He went round to a friend's house for Christmas dinner. They seem to have moved quickly on from dinner to dicing, because by three o'clock the same afternoon Lord Henry was home. In that time, he had managed to win no less than £30 at dice from his three friends—'as the devil would to blind me', he commented in retrospect. It was as much money as a manual labourer might earn in a decade. The ring was working.

Wisdom met Lord Henry as soon as he came in, was the first to hear the good news, and the first to share in it—he was given £2 'to drink', as Lord Henry put it. But Wisdom had higher ambitions than that. He now had another idea to put to his satisfied client.

'Yet will I do you more pleasure than all this,' he said. He would perform another piece of magic for him, and one which could be done rather more quickly. 'I will,' he promised, 'ere tomorrow at night, make you play as well on the lute and virginals, as any man in England.' The date, he added, was critical: this musical spell could only be cast once a year, on St Stephen's Day, 26 December. The only other requirement was a little money for expenses: another £4, he suggested. Flushed with his winnings, this sounded to Lord Henry like a good idea. Wisdom was offering him a short cut to the artistic refinement which was now expected of young aristocrats, an area in which he was embarrassingly lacking. He handed over the extra cash, and Wisdom went out to make his purchases. Christmas Day was a feast day, and normal buying and selling was suspended, but suppliers of magical equipment did not keep formal shops or regular hours, and Wisdom knew where to find them.

He returned at six o'clock the following morning laden with garish and expensive fabrics, and set about preparing the room in which the spell would be cast. He hung sheets of a green fabric called *saye* around the walls: this was a fine-textured cloth made from silk and wool, somewhat like serge. He also used a thick board of green wax to construct a makeshift altar, and set four candles burning on it. Finally, he produced two long robes of green silk, one for himself, one for Lord Henry. The two outlandishly dressed men knelt down together in front of the altar. Wisdom read aloud from a book; Lord Henry held a 'supplication', an offering of some kind. Wisdom explained that he would recite a spell which would invoke 'the god Orpheus', the mythical musician of ancient Greece. Orpheus would appear in the form of a little boy. Lord Henry would then present his offering and ask to be given the musical talents of which Wisdom had spoken. The recitation of the ritual began.

At that moment, there was a knock at the door: another piece of excellent timing. A neighbour by the name of Sir Ralph Bulmer had come by to offer greetings of the season. Henry was forced hastily to take off his robes and deal with Bulmer. After he had finally got rid of him, he returned to Wisdom and asked that they should resume. But

> then he told me that I had marred all, for the hour was past, so that it could not be done before St. Stephen's day came again.

If Lord Henry wished to impress the ladies with his lute-playing, he would have to wait another year, or learn the hard way. Possibly Bulmer's arrival was a coincidence; more likely it was prearranged, perhaps through Ninian Menville's good offices. In any case, the spell was broken.

Wisdom now tactically withdrew from the household, for Lord Henry's patience was finally beginning to fray. Matters worsened after dinner. The young nobleman now went out dicing again, but to Domingo's, a gambling-house, rather than to his friends; and this time he lost everything he had. He came home 'in a great rage', and sent Menville (whom he still did not suspect) to summon Wisdom. He accused the magician of mocking him and making a fool of him. He insisted that both his money and the contract should be returned to him. Wisdom was unfazed. If the ring had failed to work that night, he explained, most likely it was because Lord Henry 'had had to do with some woman' while wearing it; Wisdom clearly knew that Lord Henry mixed gambling with other pleasures. Such immorality would have broken the holy spell which the angels had placed on the ring. In other words, it was Lord Henry's own fault. Lord Henry would have none of it, and, as he put it, 'fell out foul with him'.

At this point, a lesser man might have walked away and counted his winnings: over £8 in cash so far, plus a month's quality accommodation. But Wisdom was not finished yet, nor had Lord Henry's faith in his powers been entirely broken. If it was simply a matter of money, he assured Lord Henry, there were other ways of finding it. Wisdom now turned again to Ninian Menville, who from now on appears ever more clearly as Wisdom's accomplice rather than as a loyal servant of the Nevilles. Wisdom had, he said, been talking to Menville, who had told him about another magician, 'a blind man which was a Jew born'. It was a potent combination. Ancient traditions linked physical blindness to spiritual perceptiveness; and Jewishness hinted at magical practices which claimed Hebrew antecedents, overlaid with the dangerous and exotic appeal of a religion whose practice was illegal in England. As a sixteenth-century proverb had it:

If one affirm he learned it of a Jew
The silly people think it must be true.

This second magician had apparently told Menville that somewhere in the Neville family estates in the North of England, there stood a wayside cross, under which lay 'a great sum of money'. Wisdom held out the prospect that he might secure this treasure trove for Lord Henry.

As with the magic ring, this idea would not have seemed as ridiculous to Lord Henry as it does to us. Some ancient barrows and mounds did indeed contain valuables. More recent treasures were buried too: in an age before banks, concealing gold and silver in the earth was a common way of keeping it safe, and who knew how many people had hidden such treasures and never lived to reclaim them? In particular, the belief that wayside crosses marked places where treasure was buried was widespread. The 1542 Act against Conjurations claimed that people searching to know 'in what place treasure of gold and silver should or might be found or had, in the earth or other secret places ... have digged up and pulled down an infinite number of Crosses within this realm'. If Lord Henry's greed was tickled by this idea, he was at least not alone in believing that X might mark the spot. Wisdom had his attention, and continued. He did not, he claimed, know how much money was buried under this particular cross, but—as luck would have it—he did have a spirit which he kept in a crystal, which he could send to find out. The spirit would not, unfortunately, be able to report back until the following morning. The delay allowed Lord Henry's temper to cool and his cupidity to grow.

In the morning, Wisdom returned with the inevitable good news. The buried treasure amounted to £2000, and in keeping with the flavour of this episode, it was in Portuguese coin— Portugal being home to the largest Jewish community surviving in western Europe. These were really substantial riches, and were almost within Lord Henry's grasp. All that was needed was the formality of collecting the money. Ever helpful, Wisdom offered to make the trip north to fetch it, accompanied by Menville. They would of course require expenses in advance, which Wisdom modestly guessed at twenty nobles, a little over £6. Lord Henry, of course, paid up. They set off on New Year's Eve. Wisdom told him that they expected to reach their destination by Twelfth Night, 6 January 1545. As a parting shot, he told Lord Henry that he would know that they had arrived safely

> by a great wind, that he would make to come into my chamber . . . which he bade me I should not be afraid of.

Laughing into their hands, and having thus bought themselves a week's grace, the two conspirators left London. Three weeks passed. Lord Henry heard nothing, and his chamber remained undisturbed. The first part of the game was over.

Eventually, Ninian Menville returned, alone. They had dug up the cross, he said, and found nothing. Wisdom had refused to return, Menville claimed, for fear that he would be beaten. Wisdom had again blamed the failure of his magic on Lord Henry, claiming—as Lord Henry put it—'that I was so vicious that he could work nothing for me'. However, in the absence of the charismatic magician, Lord Henry was not so easily pacified. He was furious, and vented his rage on Menville, whom he accused, not unreasonably, of having conspired with Wisdom to 'deceive me of my money'. For a week Menville avoided his master, while the rhythm of life in the Neville household slowly settled back to normal.

So far, there is no reason to dispute Lord Henry's account of events. The story is hardly to his own credit, although it may be that rather more money was handed over to Wisdom than he admitted. It is with the next episode that the story takes a darker twist, and Lord Henry's account becomes less trustworthy. After Menville's craven return, nothing more was heard for about a month. In the first week of Lent 1545, however, when Lord Henry was marking the penitential season by playing tennis at Westminster, he was approached quietly by Menville and Wisdom together. Wisdom was raising the stakes, because his next proposition was of a different kind from his previous ventures.

According to Lord Henry's account, Wisdom said, 'My lord, I know you love not your wife, whereby you lead an abominable life in whoredom, which will be your destruction both of body and soul.' It was not tactfully phrased, but Wisdom had put his finger on a genuine problem for Lord Henry. The issue was not merely his marital problems, nor his unsatisfactory solution to them, but his bad conscience about the matter. Lord Henry was hardly a model of pious living, but as we shall see, he did have real beliefs—if not the strength of character to act on them. Wisdom's proposed answer to Lord Henry's problem, however, was radical.

'If your wife were dead,' he said, 'then might you choose one, which you might find in your heart to love, and by that means lead an honest and a godly life. And here I have a book, wherewith I can dispatch her, and not known but that she died of God's hand.' And as he brandished this devilish spell-book, he added, incongruously: 'This, I think, shall be the best way for you, for she (good lady) is sure to go to heaven.'

According to his own account, Lord Henry was utterly horrified by this suggestion, and sent the two of them packing, 'thinking nothing less than that they would have gone about any such practice'. Three weeks later, on Sunday 15 March 1545, he met them again—by chance, he claimed—at Moorgate, on the northern edge of London. Wisdom now assured him that the deed was done. A fatal spell had already been placed on Lord Henry's wife, and also—and this is the first time we hear of this—on his father, the earl. It was, Wisdom said, only a matter of time before both of them died, and Lord Henry could find a new wife to go with his new title. Lord Henry again claimed to have been astonished and horrified, and to have cursed the day he met either of them. 'It will be thought that it came by my procurement,' he protested—and it will indeed. In prison in 1546, pleading for his life, this was the one part of his story that he changed. In a letter written in his own hand to Secretary Paget, apparently after his full confession, Lord Henry repeated his claim that the idea had been Wisdom's, but admitted that he had consented at least to the murder of Lady Anne. This seems a good deal more likely. It would have been odd for Wisdom to have set about such an activity unilaterally, and it also explains the 'chance' meeting at Moorgate. Moreover, Lord Henry admitted to Paget that he had been persuaded by Wisdom's splendid piece of casuistry: a win–win scenario in which Lady Anne died and went to heaven, and Lord Henry could marry a woman he loved.

So the plan seems to have had Lord Henry's consent, in part at least. However, it does seem that he lost his nerve once it was clear that Wisdom had actually cast the spell. Perhaps it was the inclusion of his father which unnerved him; or perhaps an idea which sounded compelling when the magician was explaining it seemed rather different after a few guilt-wracked days and nights waiting for bad news from the North or from Lady Anne's servants. In any case, it seems likely that he really did fall out with Wisdom and Menville on 15 March, for he cited several witnesses to that effect. The following day, Menville came crawling back. He begged Lord Henry to look kindly on him, and 'cloaked . . . his fault with many fair words'. It took a little work, but as Menville must have known, Lord Henry was not a man to dig his heels in when under pressure. Lord Henry was, sensibly enough, directing his fury chiefly at Wisdom, and so Menville now promised to fetch Wisdom so that he could be arrested and face the rigour of the law.

Menville set out, but quickly returned alone. Wisdom, he claimed, was bound to his bed by a spirit and could not move. However, Lord Henry's underexercised powers of scepticism were now finally becoming aroused. He resolved to go to Wisdom's house himself and confront him. He set out at six o'clock the following morning, accompanied by Menville and several others from the Neville household: a dawn raid. As they were on their way, they met Wisdom himself 'coming a great pace, and as soon as he saw me he began to halt and draw his leg after him'. Possibly Wisdom, forewarned, was trying to escape London; more likely, he was coming to seize control of the situation once more, trusting in his ability to bamboozle his noble client. But not even Lord Henry was now going to be fooled by a stage limp. His posse seized Wisdom, and Lord Henry 'gave him a great blow, saying his halting should not save him'. They dragged the magician out of the City into the fields beyond Moorgate. He struggled, but Lord Henry took a dagger from one of his servants and made as if to stab the prisoner. He claimed he was only prevented from doing so by the servant, who sensibly intervened: Lord Henry did not need to add a murder charge to his other troubles. Instead, he sent Wisdom back to the Neville household under guard, while Lord Henry and Menville went on to the duke of Suffolk's residence, with the intention—or so he claimed—of laying the whole affair before the duke. The game was finally over.

However, Lord Henry claimed that he was denied access to the duke, who was very sick. Again, this part of Lord Henry's account invites some scepticism. The duke was indeed sick, and he was to die five months later, but in March 1545 he was not yet so incapacitated as to be unable to receive visitors. This is also the one part of Lord Henry's account which we know Wisdom actively disputed. More importantly, however, Lord Henry would have thought twice before implicating himself, whatever his fury at Wisdom. This failed attempt to involve the duke is the sort of spurious detail which Lord Henry might well have concocted later to put himself in a good light—that he had tried, but failed, to contact the authorities. He certainly emphasized this point in his confession. Even so, he admitted that he had in fact returned home without having spoken about the matter to anyone. Instead, he again confronted Wisdom, declaring that he would never rest until the magician was hanged.

Wisdom, however, pointed out what Lord Henry had probably already realized: that Lord Henry was now deeply entangled in Wisdom's activities and could not bring him down without also condemning himself. It was true. Wisdom had, with Lord Henry's connivance, broken almost every clause of the Act against Conjurations. He had invoked spirits, he had used enchantment to win riches, he had manufactured a magical artefact, he had (supposedly) dug up a cross to find hidden treasure, and he had used magic to kill. The only substantive offence under the Act which he had *not* committed was to concoct a love potion; that, perhaps, would have followed once Lord Henry was a single man again. Under the terms of the Act, Lord Henry was as guilty as Wisdom. Having explained the problem, Wisdom presented Lord Henry with the only possible solution:

> Then Menville and he kneeled both upon their knees before me, and with their crafty persuasions brought me in such a fear that I let them both go, charging Wisdom that he should never come in my sight.

Menville was sent to the family's country estates. Lord Henry claimed that he never saw either of them again.

Wisdom vanished—for the time being, at least. The fates of the other participants are easier to trace.

Needless to say, neither Earl Ralph nor Lady Anne died. Ninian Menville did what he had done when he had been in trouble previously: he appealed to Lord Henry's mother, Countess Katherine. A month after Menville and Lord Henry finally parted company, Countess Katherine wrote a personal letter of recommendation to the earl of Shrewsbury, the King's lieutenant in the North, asking him to appoint Menville to a military captaincy. Menville was, she claimed, 'very desirous to serve the King's majesty on the Borders'. Lord Henry turned his attention to soldiering in the North as well, joining in a substantial raid which was mounted into Scotland in the autumn of 1545. The following July he was sent as part of an embassy to France. Not long afterwards, however, the secret finally came out. There is little sign of how the story broke. All we know is that by 1 October 1546, when Lord Henry was already under arrest, members of the Privy Council were being badgered by suitors wishing to speak to the prisoner. His gambling debts had certainly not gone away in the meantime, and it may be that they had overtaken him: for the Fleet Prison, where he was thrown, was principally for debtors. Perhaps a creditor had found out part of the story and had tried to blackmail the hapless youngster.

It was a dangerous time for such a story to break, because the autumn of 1546 was feverish with political tension. Henry VIII was slowly dying—a fact which was obvious to all England, although to say so aloud was high treason. The prince of Wales, Edward, was not quite 9 years old. With a minority government obviously approaching, 1546 was a year of

murderous plots and counter-plots, rumours and prophecies, as political factions positioned themselves to dominate
the new regime. The old King himself was entering his
final, vicious spasm of bloodletting. That winter, the earl of
Surrey—one of England's most prominent young noblemen,
and a friend of Lord Henry's—would die a traitor's death after
a shocking arrest and whirlwind trial. It was not a good time
to be accused of plotting the murder of an earl by witchcraft.
Lord Henry did the only thing he sensibly could, and made
a full and grovelling confession. This made it clear that the
stability of the country was not at stake, and so probably
saved his life. It also provided us with a marvellously detailed
account.

Following the confession, the whole conspiracy was
rounded up. Menville and the servant George Stafford were
quickly imprisoned; so too, apparently, was Wisdom himself.
Secretary Paget, in charge of the case, interviewed Lord
Henry personally on at least two occasions. He also received
a series of wretched letters in which Lord Henry pleaded for
his life, a life which he admitted he had forfeited twenty times
over. If the desperate tone of the letters had not made it clear
that Lord Henry was no threat to the state, their abysmal
handwriting would have done so. Lord Henry's spelling and
penmanship were very eccentric indeed, even by the standards of sixteenth-century aristocrats; testament to a man
with neither the education nor the sophistication to be taken
very seriously at court. Moreover, he was plainly terrified.
He begged Paget to deal with his case personally, so that he
might be spared the ordeal of examination before the full Privy
Council. He begged for his family to be spared the shame
of an execution. He promised to be a reformed character,
and to 'live with that good lady my wife to the contentation
of God and all the world'. He blamed his crimes on lack

1. One of the letters which Lord Henry wrote to Sir William Paget from prison. The spidery handwriting and eccentric spelling testify to his limited education.

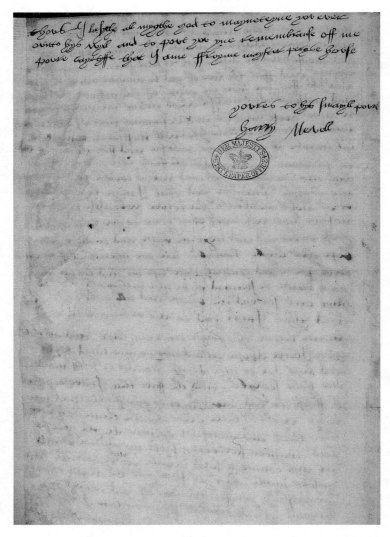

1. (*Continued*)

of wit, on lack of counsel, on his youth, on the Devil and—particularly—on Wisdom and Menville. (He insisted, however, that Stafford, his 'assured friend', was innocent; he may even have been right.) What may have had more impact, his father and his wife, his supposed victims, both also intervened on his behalf.

Of course, the English aristocracy being what it is, the whole affair ended happily. Lord Henry spent a few bleak months in prison. However, after the old King finally died in January 1547 and the new regime of Edward VI settled itself into place, there was a marked easing of tension and a temporary end to political bloodshed. Lord Henry seems to have been a beneficiary of this change of mood. He was released in March 1547, with the comment that his crimes had not been so grave as they had at first appeared. At the same time, the Privy Council asked the earl, Lord Henry's father, to clear his son's debts so that, as they put it, 'he may begin the world again'. When the earl agreed, the government even helped by deferring for three years Lord Henry's debts to the Crown, a total of £437. Lord Henry slowly resumed his normal place in society. A line was definitively drawn under the affair by the Parliament which met in December 1547. It passed not only a general pardon, as was customary, but also a general Act of Repeal, abolishing all the new felonies which had been created by Henry VIII's murderous legislative activism. The Act against Conjurations was swept away almost by default.

Lord Henry was not so foolish as to become entangled with London's underworld again, but he did not lose his faith in get-rich-quick schemes. In April 1549, the old earl finally died, and Lord Henry became the fifth earl of Westmorland. But his inheritance did not turn out to be the simple passport to riches he had imagined. This, at least, is the implication of a breathlessly excited entry in King Edward VI's private journal, which claims that in 1549 the new earl of Westmorland had plotted to seize some of the Neville family treasure, held at Middleham in Yorkshire; to have robbed his mother (of what, we are not told); and to have sold £200 worth of land. But it was not all about cashflow. He was allegedly also preparing to make a populist and illegal proclamation against the debasing of the coinage. This was the kind of thing you did if you were trying to start a rebellion; and it was a year when almost every corner of England saw risings, disturbances, and illegal assemblies triggered by resentment against inflation, taxation, enclosure of common land, and bewildering religious change. As it was, the dean of Durham Cathedral got wind of this particular plot, stopped it in its tracks, and ensured that no one other than the King's inner circle found out. The government, it seems, still recognized that Henry Neville was not really a very dangerous man.

Thereafter, he settled down into a moderately distinguished nobleman's career. He sat briefly on the Privy Council, led a couple of embassies to Scotland, and served as Lord Lieutenant in the North. He managed to keep out of trouble during the bewildering political changes of the 1550s. When King Edward died in 1553, his ministers tried to carry out his quixotic wish to install Jane Grey as queen instead of Mary Tudor, but Mary mounted a successful coup; Jane Grey was imprisoned and, eventually, executed. Earl Henry played both sides, in the finest Neville tradition. When the dust had cleared and Mary was in control, she thanked him (through gritted teeth?) for the 'coldness' with which he had upheld Jane's title. Mary now returned England to Catholic orthodoxy, and sealed this decision by marrying her cousin Philip, who would shortly become King of Spain. It seems likely that

Earl Henry liked neither her faith nor her husband, but he served them loyally, again principally on the Scottish borders. In 1557 he even swallowed his pride and allowed a Scottish nobleman to taunt him for being a 'Spaniard'. However, when Mary herself died, childless, in 1558, to be succeeded by her half-sister Elizabeth, Earl Henry was ready to serve this new regime too. Elizabeth, a Protestant, was promptly declared Supreme Governor of the Church, and Earl Henry readily took part in ensuring that her subjects swore to acknowledge this new title. There was even a rumour—completely groundless—that the new Queen was contemplating him as a possible husband.

He did not marry royalty, but the marital unhappiness of which he had complained in 1545 did end as he had hoped. Lady Anne died in or after 1549; her death, coinciding as it nearly did with Earl Ralph's, must have stirred guilty and embarrassing memories for Lord Henry. He went on to marry twice more—scandalously, his second and third wives were sisters. However, his own health was uncertain by the mid-1550s. When war with Scotland threatened in 1557, he was sent north to negotiate, and did so, but his companions worried that he was 'pained with his old disease'; and he was making brave oaths to serve his sovereign 'while life lasted', which were only a little premature. He died on 10 February 1564, a little way short of his fortieth birthday. Charles, his son by Lady Anne, became the sixth earl. He was to become notorious as one of the leaders of a rebellion against Queen Elizabeth in 1569.

Ninian Menville was not nearly so distinguished a figure, but we know a surprising amount about his subsequent career too, for he has left a trail of self-promotion and treachery through the archives. We do not know how or when he was freed from prison—perhaps he was released along with

2. The effigy of Henry Neville, fifth earl of Westmorland, on his tomb in Staindrop Church, County Durham. The tomb was commissioned during his lifetime and may be a realistic likeness.

3. The effigy of Anne, Lady Neville (née Manners) from the same tomb.

his former master—but we do know he was free by the late summer of 1547, for on 10 September he fought at the Battle of Pinkie, when an English army invading Scotland won a bloody victory over one of the largest Scottish hosts ever assembled. We next meet him in 1550, acting as an agent provocateur for the government. He wrote a series of letters to Bishop Tunstall of Durham, a tenacious religious conservative whom the fervently Protestant regime was trying to remove. In these letters Menville hinted darkly at plans for a rebellion in the North of England in which he hoped Tunstall might join. Eventually Tunstall was lured into expressing some unguarded sentiments in reply, and Menville immediately laid the entire correspondence before the Privy Council. These letters were the pretext on which Tunstall was imprisoned and eventually deprived of his bishopric.

Menville surfaces twice more in the historical record. In 1553, during the turbulent weeks following Queen Mary's accession, he was summoned before the Privy Council: for what reason we do not know, although by now it is clear that he was a man who was good at making enemies. We know rather more about his activities in 1559–60, when England once again became involved in a war in Scotland, and Elizabeth I's shaky regime looked for help from anyone who might claim expertise in the northern kingdom's affairs. In August 1559 Menville wrote to William Cecil, Elizabeth's chief minister, offering information and his own services. He gave a careful background report on the master of Maxwell, one of the Scottish nobles with whom the English were negotiating. He also claimed to be closely acquainted with many other key Scottish lords and gentlemen, and to be able to provide maps of important military sites in Scotland. He urged Cecil to ensure that any messages sent north should be sent in code, for security, and modestly insisted that he himself was the only man who could be trusted to carry them safely. In fact, the style and much of the substance of Menville's advice was out of date; he was still fighting the last war. However, his efforts at self-promotion were not wasted. In October 1559, the government sent him to the Border, escorting a high-profile Scottish defector. He spent the winter in Newcastle upon Tyne, and in February 1560, he was finally given a command: as captain of the *Marie Flower*, a ship in the small English navy then stationed off the north-east coast.

We know nothing more about Menville's military career, and it is even possible that he was killed during the sharp fighting which followed during the spring and summer of 1560. That his character had not changed, however, is plain. On 28 November 1559, when stationed in Newcastle, he wrote to the English regime's principal agents in the North with a complaint against the splendidly named Albany Fetherstonhalf. Fetherstonhalf had fallen into a dispute with Menville over a gold chain worth £29, and another £5 in cash. Menville was looking for support from friends in high places to settle the matter. He called on the earl of Northumberland's assistance, and also hinted that the Queen's favourite, Robert Dudley, might intervene on his behalf. It is striking, however, that in none of this correspondence did he give any hint of a relationship with that other powerful northern earl, Westmorland. It seems that Ninian Menville and his old master had no wish to renew their acquaintance.

What, then, are we to make of the troubles of Henry, Lord Neville? It is a story which can be read on several levels. The simplest is to see it as a cautionary tale for aristocrats who have more money than sense: they will always attract the attention of people such as Wisdom who will help them to redress that balance. It is perhaps also a parable about the eclipse of the old nobility in Tudor England, in which the low-born, ruthless, and clever were outmanoeuvring those who depended more on their pedigrees than their wits. However, this remarkable and uniquely detailed tale has some more specific and more surprising things to say to us, and it unlocks further stories just as revealing. Those stories centre around the most enigmatic figure in Lord Henry's story, and the one whose subsequent career is not laid out for all to see in the State Papers: Wisdom, the sorcerer.

2

The Physician

Wнo was Wisdom? He vanishes from Lord Henry's story without trace, as suddenly as he appears in it. The records of Lord Henry's arrest, trial, and release make no mention of his fate. When I first read this case, and saw the way Lord Henry used only the single name 'Wisdom', I assumed that this was a sorcerer's *nom de guerre*. But one clue which Lord Henry left unlocks the secret for us. After he met Wisdom and Menville on 15 March 1545, and learned that the fatal spells had been cast, Lord Henry sent for Wisdom's father. He spoke to the older man in the fields beyond Moorgate, where he would come close to murdering Wisdom the next day, and told him that 'that villain thy son hath gone about to destroy my father and my wife'. Wisdom's father professed to be shocked, condemned his son's actions, and claimed he had nothing to do with the matter. Lord Henry mentioned this encounter because he hoped, rather forlornly, that Wisdom's father might testify in his favour. But in doing so he referred to the man, in passing, as 'old Wisdom'. That might imply that he did not know either man's real name, but it is more likely that 'Wisdom' was not a pseudonym after all.

'Wisdom' was not a common surname in Tudor England, and if we bring in two other scraps of information—that Wisdom the sorcerer had a day job as a physician, as he told Lord Henry, and that he had a father also living in London— it is possible to identify our man. There was a well-known father-and-son team of medical practitioners in London in the early 1540s named John and Gregory Wisdom. The younger man, Gregory Wisdom, is the obvious candidate to be our sorcerer, and as we shall see, there is corroborative evidence which places the identification beyond reasonable doubt. It turns out that Gregory Wisdom's public and private careers can shed light not only on his part in the Neville affair, but also on the many other worlds in which he moved.

To understand who the Wisdoms were, we need to begin with their profession. In theory, the English medical profession in the sixteenth century was an orderly, hierarchical system in which everybody had their role and knew their place. In practice, this rigid system was a fiction which the medical establishment was trying, and largely failing, to impose on a vibrant, turbulent, and disreputable world of medical practice. The chaos was all the worse because of the appearance of a new and terrifying disease, in the face of which the profession was helpless. It is no surprise that we find John and Gregory Wisdom at the centre of this maelstrom, trying to claw their way up the hierarchy and, in the process, doing their part to pull it down.

The most fundamental division in the medical profession was that between trained (and exclusively male) professionals, and the great mass of amateurs: white witches, cunningfolk, dabblers, and good neighbours. We know very little about the hidden world of informal medicine, a world in which skills were self-taught or handed down from mother to daughter; only that this was how most men and women in England received what little medical care they did. The trained professionals were expensive, confined to the cities, and very few in number. While their learning might be impressive, they were no less likely to kill their patients than the common healers whom they despised. The learned medics were themselves divided into three supposedly distinct professions. There were the apothecaries, who were the pharmacists of the sixteenth century, specialists in formulating and preparing medicines— as well as, it was widely believed, magical potions and deadly poisons. They are not, however, directly relevant to our story, unlike the two other branches of respectable medicine: surgeons and physicians.

Physicians were the self-appointed princes of early modern medicine: university-educated bearers of the traditions of ancient Greece and Rome. This was a tradition which ascribed most illness to imbalances between the 'humours' in the body—blood, phlegm, and two varieties of bile. In particular, this tradition held that fever was caused by an excess of blood, the humour which was understood to be a form of fire. Bleeding patients was one of the physician's most versatile treatments—and if a person is bled severely enough, it will indeed temporarily reduce a fever, although it may well also be fatal. The physician's particular forte, however, was diagnosis: the difficult art of discerning the true nature of an illness beneath the mess of symptoms, an art made more difficult by learned physic's determination to fit diseases to the categories bequeathed by the ancients. The physician's role was to examine the patient, to interrogate, to feel the pulse, to listen to the breath, and to sniff the urine ('piss-prophets', disrespectful patients called them); and then to pronounce a diagnosis and recommend a treatment, if any could be found. Even if you simply had a cold, it was said, a physician would 'tell you your malady in Greek'. He would then have an apothecary prepare the medicines, treatments which were usually at least as unpleasant as the disease.

The physicians' calling, then, was sombre, ineffectual, and expensive. The expense they worked particularly hard to maintain. They were governed and protected by the Royal College of Physicians, a trade guild created in 1518 with the explicit aims of confining the practice of physic to university-trained men; of excluding and prosecuting others who tried to muscle in on the business; and so of keeping prices high. The College made physicians rich, but it did not make them loved. Bishop Latimer complained in 1552 that 'physic is a remedy prepared only for rich folks'. A century later, Archbishop Sancroft rued his treatment at the hands of London's physicians: 'a man cannot die good cheap here'. Yet another bishop, John Earle, was less phlegmatic. A physician, he wrote, is 'a very brother to the worms, for they both breed out of man's corruption. ... The best cure he has done is upon his own purse, which from a lean sickliness he has made lusty.' Clerical pronouncements like this were meant to shame the profession: in fact, they may simply have helped to attract young men looking to make their fortunes.

The third branch of the profession was the surgeons. They had their own trade association, created by 1540, which linked them with barbers. That link is a sign that surgery was not a gentlemanly profession. It was a craft requiring manual skill, physical strength, and moral courage rather than profound learning. Our modern image of the barber-surgeon is a brutal one, not helped by some of the contemporary depictions of surgeons at work, but this is not entirely fair. In theory, a distinction was maintained between barbers and surgeons; and sixteenth-century surgery was not quite so lethal a prospect as it might seem. In an age before antisepsis or blood transfusions, surgeons were well aware that anything like a major operation would almost always be fatal. Killing too many patients was bad for business. Moreover, in an age where the best painkiller available was a recent invention called brandy, patients were unenthusiastic about subjecting themselves to

4. A German woodcut of surgeons at work, 1517.

the knife. Most surgeons therefore stuck to those procedures which they could perform relatively safely and (equally importantly, for many patients) relatively quickly. These ranged from dental extractions, through the setting of broken bones, to more drastic measures like amputation—which, for all its obvious disadvantages, was a tolerably safe way of dealing with life-threatening conditions such as gangrene.

Physicians, of course, looked down on surgeons, and in theory the boundary between the two specialisms was clear.

Surgery was defined as treatment of the surface of a patient's body; the innards were a physician's territory. Bishop Earle again provides the *bon mot*: a surgeon, he wrote, 'differs from a physician, as a sore does from a disease'. The physician 'distempers you within, and the other blisters you without'. His talk of sores and blisters makes an important point: since the surface of the body was their province, surgeons also dealt in burns, scalds, and skin diseases.

However, the distinctions between physician, surgeon, and apothecary were never so rigid as purists would have liked. Even fastidious specialists could hardly avoid trespassing on one another's domains. In particular, the more gifted and ambitious surgeons might encroach on the physicians' monopoly, if faced with conditions which the physicians seemed helpless to remedy. This was particularly the case if they confronted diseases and injuries which did not respect the neat distinction between external and internal afflictions. In the early sixteenth century, these problems were acutely posed by an alarming new disease which, it seemed, corrupted the surface of the body while also rotting it from within: the disease which was then called the 'great pox', or the 'French disease', and which we know as syphilis.

The origins of syphilis are unknown—it is possible, but no more than possible, that Columbus' men brought it back from the New World in 1493. What is known is that the first confirmed cases in Europe appeared in Italy in 1494, and it spread with frightening speed thereafter, in an epidemic eerily similar to the spread of AIDS in modern times. This was a virulent, fatal but slow-acting sexually transmitted disease, which could be treated (up to a point) but could not be cured. Like AIDS, it had its share of celebrity victims— although Henry VIII was probably not one of them. And like AIDS, the pox initially baffled the medical establishment.

5. Dry-stove treatment for syphilis, as illustrated in a
seventeenth-century engraving.

The ancient medical writers who were the foundation of
learned physic made no mention of this disease, although
plenty of physicians tried to discover it in their works. Early in
the epidemic doctors were reduced to such harmless and futile
suggestions as that patients shave their heads. The harmless-
ness, at least, did not last long. The main treatment for the pox
which learned medicine eventually developed was a hellish
device known as the 'dry stove'. This was a large barrel in
which the unfortunate patient was enclosed. The bottom of
the barrel was perforated and it was then placed on a bed
of hot stones and sand. The patient, who would be made
to fast beforehand, would endure these cramped and super-
heated conditions for an hour or two at a time, sometimes

twice a day for as much as a week. The purpose of this torture was to make the patient sweat copiously, which—it was hoped—would expel the noxious humours which caused the disease. The treatment was ineffective and extremely unpleasant. All of which meant that the pox represented a ghastly opportunity for innovative doctors (or charlatans) who were able to come up with alternatives which were (or seemed) effective.

The surgeons were ideally placed to exploit this opportunity. It helped that skin lesions, which were amongst the most painful and horrific symptoms of the pox, were a problem which fell in surgical territory, and surgeons could adapt existing treatments for skin disease to confront this new problem. Equally importantly, the surgeons' experience-based approach to medicine meant that they were less committed to the package of medical ideas inherited from the ancients, and were more willing to contemplate fashionable new treatments. In particular, they were more open to the use of chemical or alchemical medicine. This dangerous, powerful tradition looked less to the ancient world than to learned Arabic medicine (the word 'alchemy' itself has Arabic roots). It also drew on a range of Christian experimentalists and occultists ranging from the English friar Roger Bacon to the sinister, brilliant Swiss sorcerer-physician who called himself Paracelsus. Alchemical medicine had long used mercury—that mysterious liquid metal—as a treatment for conditions such as lice and scabies: it was quickly adapted for use against syphilis. Ointments based on mercury were applied sparingly to the patient's syphilitic lesions over the course of several days, often in an environment made as hot as possible. Mercury vapour was also inhaled. The treatment was extremely painful and also very dangerous—mercury is toxic, and some patients were killed by it—but it was also not wholly ineffective. It certainly made them salivate and vomit copiously, which masked, if it did not ease, the symptoms of the pox.

Another, less respectable treatment was taken from the guaiacum trees of the Caribbean. Lotions based on the sap or, more commonly, the pulverized wood of the tree were applied to the patient's skin, and a more watery version could be drunk. This, too, could sometimes help, partly but perhaps not only because the violent fever it provoked could mask the symptoms for a while. But learned physicians loathed guaiacum. It was a treatment with no ancient warrant, and, worse, with no theoretical explanation of why it might work. Guaiacum was in short supply and, for most patients, prohibitively expensive, but it nevertheless became a cause célèbre for those who opposed learned medicine's monopolies. The result was that the professional battlelines only hardened. Physicians despised those who experimented with such methods as 'empirics', who reduced medicine to something lumpishly practical and had no understanding of what they were doing. The 'empirics', and their patients, replied that understanding disease mattered less than curing it.

The surgeons were in the front line of the war against the pox for other reasons. Surgery as a specialism had always had a close relationship with the military: early modern armies and navies abundantly produced the kinds of injuries which needed a surgeon's rough-and-ready talents. This meant that London's surgeons were concentrated in those parts of the city where soldiers and sailors were to be found—the docks to the east, and Holborn and Smithfield to the west. This mattered because armies and navies were also one of the main vectors for transmitting the pox across Europe. Nor were the surgeons the only civilians looking to make a living from the military: the same areas were well provided with prostitutes, and therefore also with venereal disease. And barber shops, as exclusively male environments, were an obvious port of call for men needing sexual advice of all kinds, especially when they were next door to brothels. The result was a whole military-surgical-sexual ecosystem which ensured that venereal disease had long been a specialty for surgeons, and that the niceties of the professional divide with the physicians would be trampled.

Here we can return to the Wisdoms. As the syphilis epidemic spread, medical turf wars were breaking out across Europe. In England, the crisis came after the Barber-Surgeon's Company was formally licensed in 1540. The respectable surgeons at the head of the new Company were committed to defending the status quo, and they joined with the Royal College of Physicians in a set of exemplary prosecutions of those surgeons who were breaking professional boundaries. On 6 July 1541, with the Royal College's backing, a surgeon named Otwell Wylde brought a case against five medics whom he accused of practising 'the mystery of physic' in London without a licence for the eleven months since the new Company's creation. He asked the court to fine the men £55 each (£5 a month) for un-licensed practice, with half of the fine going (through Wylde) to the Royal College of Physicians. Two of the defendants were John and Gregory Wisdom.

Three of the cases were quickly settled. The charges against Gregory Wisdom and one of the others were apparently dropped, and a third man, an apothecary, pleaded guilty and was dismissed with a fine of two marks (a little over a pound). The two principal cases, however, were those against a Frenchman named John Lyster, and John Wisdom of the parish of St Stephen Coleman Street, London. John Wisdom was described in the indictment as a surgeon. How-ever, he and his sons were not actually members of the

Barber-Surgeons' Company, but of another, less dignified London livery: the Painter-Stainers' Company. The idea of painters and decorators dabbling in medicine might seem alarming, but it was not uncommon. Painter-stainers were responsible for mixing their own paints, and so were the closest thing that London had to a professional association of chemists. When dealing with preparations such as mercury, this was valuable expertise. The overlap with medicine was hardly respectable, but it was clear.

Their cases came to trial at the Lord Mayor's court in December, and were concluded at the beginning of February 1542. Both men were found guilty, although the fines were reduced to £10 for John Wisdom and £30 for Lyster. They paid before the end of the month, and both men were even given a small refund by the Royal College for their prompt submission. The College clearly took the case extremely seriously, making a more detailed record of these events than of anything else that decade. In January 1542, before the final judgement was pronounced, the officials of the College oversaw the public burning of medicines confiscated from the defendants. Throughout, the College's records refer to Wisdom and Lyster, contemptuously, as 'empirics'. The establishment seemed to have won.

But neither man accepted defeat. Lyster appealed to the City of London's authorities for help, and John Wisdom appealed directly to King Henry VIII. Both relied on testimonials from satisfied patients, and in Wisdom's case at least, the result was spectacular. On 1 June 1542, the Lord Chancellor issued letters patent in the King's name which declared that Otwell Wylde's lawsuit had been 'instigated and provoked by divers evil disposed persons maliciously stomached against the said John Wisdom'—an extraordinary swipe at the Royal College. The King was further made to state that Wisdom had 'done many and great cures to divers and sundry our subjects'. Wisdom was pardoned and the result of the earlier lawsuit overturned. There is no evidence he ever got his money back, but he did get something much more valuable. The King gave both John Wisdom, and his son Gregory, an unrestricted licence to practise physic anywhere in England. Henry VIII, having given the Royal College its monopoly, was now taking it away.

What these 'great cures' were is not specified, but it seems certain that syphilis was at the heart of the case. The government was alarmed about the disease, as was the King himself, whether or not he was a sufferer. Twice around this time, in 1535 and (rather more seriously) in 1546, attempts were made to suppress London's main licensed brothels in Southwark, in response to outbreaks of the pox there—although closure merely dispersed the prostitutes who had worked there and so spread the disease still further.

The royal grant made to the Wisdoms was the first of its kind, but it was not the last. Several other such unrestricted licences were granted to 'empirics' over the next year, and when Parliament next met, in 1543, it undermined the Royal College's monopoly more systematically. The Act then passed was nicknamed the 'Quacks' Charter' by the physicians' establishment, for it granted a sweeping right for 'empirics' of all kinds to practice their trade untroubled by the Royal College. It condemned the medical establishment for extorting money from the poor and for having 'sued troubled and vexed divers honest persons' who had treated the poor for free. And while the Act did not explicitly cite the pox epidemic, its description of the symptoms which unlicensed physicians were treating makes it plain what diseases were meant. It spoke of 'uncomes' and 'saucelin' (swellings, pustules, and inflammations) on the face and hands, 'morphew' (discoloured skin lesions), and 'strangury' (slow and painful urination), conditions which made the poor 'rot and perish to death'. In the face of a public health emergency, the establishment's self-interest could not be allowed to keep out skilled men like the Wisdoms.

After this confrontation, both John and Gregory Wisdom continued to practise. When Gregory Wisdom proudly declared to Henry, Lord Neville that he was a 'physician', he was telling a half-truth. He had no qualifications as such, and his only formal status was his membership of the Painter-Stainers' Company. But he did have a royal grant, a grant on which he and his father were to trade for much of the rest of their lives. Both still aspired to be accepted by the Royal College of Physicians. The grant from Henry VIII was perfectly valid, but the Royal College continued to pester them, and being admitted to its ranks would confer considerable status. In 1553 John Wisdom applied, but was rejected along with several others: the College was still smarting from its defeat of a decade earlier. In 1552, the College's future president John Caius, the greatest English physician of his generation, wrote scathingly of a profession overrun by charlatans. 'Be so good to your bodies,' he appealed to the public, 'as you are to your shoes': choose a doctor with at least the care that one would choose a shoemaker. Instead, he lamented, the English turned to quacks claiming to be Indians, Egyptians, or Jews, selling potions 'as though they were made of the sun, moon or stars', but whose ingredients were in truth 'so filthy, that I am ashamed to name them'. Or if not, they would turn to 'simple women, carpenters, pewterers, braziers, soapball-sellers, poulterers, hostellers' or—last and perhaps worst of all—'painters'.

His complaint was heard in 1553 when Parliament repealed the Quacks' Charter and placed the barber-surgeons and the apothecaries under the Royal College's own control. The syphilis crisis had barely abated, but the newly unified medical establishment reasserted itself forcefully. The surgeon Thomas Gale painted a horrifying pen-portrait of the effects of unlicensed medical practice: in 1562, he claimed, he had seen over three hundred patients at St Thomas' and St Bartholomew's Hospitals in London who had been maimed or crippled by quack medicine. The culprits were not honest empirics, but charlatans and crooks; worst of all, many of them were women, most of whom he clearly believed were witches. The physician John Securis, from his loftier perch, was sniffier. He was at least honest enough to admit that he disliked unlicensed medicine because it might 'hinder and defraud us of our lawful stipend and gains'. He was contemptuous of those who claimed to be physicians but knew no Latin; as we shall see, this included the Wisdoms. (Securis complained, rather endearingly, that if such people could practice medicine, 'then were it a great folly for us ... to break our brains in reading so many authors'.) But he also insisted that quacks could be lethal. Referring to the empirics' fondness for purgatives (drugs which provoked diarrhoea and vomiting—the original detox), Securis warned: 'They purge so much and so often, that they purge many times as well the soul out of the body, as the money out of the purse.'

In this environment, it is no surprise that the upstart painters John and Gregory Wisdom found their ascent blocked. John invested cannily in property, and attained a position of some honour within the Painter-Stainers' Company. In 1549, he led a consortium of fourteen painter-stainers (including both his sons) who took over the lease of

Painters' Hall, the Company's premises. But while this was
gratifying, and no doubt lucrative, it brought him no closer to
medical respectability. When John Wisdom drew up his will
in 1559 (he died three years later, in 1562) he was still balanced
between two worlds. He was still living where he had been for
twenty years or more, in the London parish of St Stephen's
Coleman Street, just inside the City walls, next to Moorgate.
His will, unusually, did not mention his profession. He neither wished to claim to be a painter-stainer, nor dared claim to
be a physician. His actual practice of physic is unmistakable:
one of his servants was bequeathed a three-volume set of the
works of Galen, greatest of the ancient physicians, along with
a guide to medicinal herbs. But this servant's name—Richard
Pincter, that is, 'Painter'—is a reminder of the circles John
Wisdom had really moved in. It took more than books to
become a physician.

Gregory Wisdom, too, remained a freelance physician for
the time being. He was accepted by some of those whom he
wanted to see as his peers. When one of Queen Elizabeth
I's surgeons died in 1566, he named Gregory Wisdom as one
of the overseers of his will. But whatever the surgeons might
think, Wisdom was still excluded from the top table. In 1570
he clashed with Hector Nuñez, a Portuguese Jew who had
become part of the London medical establishment since his
arrival in 1549, and who now served some of the Queen's most
exalted courtiers as a physician and as a spy. Nuñez accused
Gregory of 'wicked and ignorant conduct': specifically, he
disagreed with Wisdom's decision to administer an enema to a
patient, a treatment which strayed across the barrier between
external and internal medicine and so violated the physicians'
privileges. The Royal College solemnly heard the case, and
threatened Wisdom with a £6 fine and imprisonment, but
in the event Nuñez was unable to produce any evidence.

Whether this was personal animosity or professional disagreement, the case was a reminder that Wisdom's practice was barely suffered: the records again describe him with official contempt as 'Gregory Wisdom, empiric'.

Twelve years later he finally came in from the cold. In 1582 Gregory Wisdom, now presumably in his sixties, was admitted to the Royal College of Physicians as a licentiate, the lowest grade of member. The records of his admission are curt, but they are enough to make it plain how unusual the case was. It was more than twenty years since a man with no university training had been admitted to the Royal College, and even then it had been unusual: the last non-university man before Wisdom had been specifically restricted to one narrow branch of medicine (the external treatment of eye disease) that was barely distinguishable from mere surgery. Wisdom did not face any conditions of that nature, but other hurdles were put in his way. Bluntly, if the College was going to admit this man, it was at least going to make him pay. Initially, the College proposed that he make an unspecified, but large, one-off donation and then commit to pay £8 per year for the rest of his life. After some negotiation, this was reduced to a £5 joining fee and a £4 annual payment—still many times the sum expected from the average licentiate, and a substantial slice of Wisdom's wealth. (He was assessed for taxes that year as owning property worth £15, although this was likely an underestimate.) Wisdom did, however, eventually secure the precious letters patent which declared in the Royal College's name that 'the worthy man Gregory Wisdom . . . who has for long practised medicine' was granted 'the free faculty and licence to employ and practise the science and art of medicine'. Even then, there was a sting in the tail. As well as specifying his hefty annual subscription, the letters patent demanded that 'in all his actions he is to preserve the authority of the College'—a requirement which was not a part of the standard form. Even if he had mellowed with age, the physicians knew they were dealing with a slippery customer. Less than three weeks later, the Royal College was scandalized by an extraordinary burst of unprovoked temper from Wisdom's former enemy Hector Nuñez, directed at one of the College's officials; the incident was put down to 'a disturbed mental state', a state which may not have been helped by the arrival of the new licentiate.

Gregory Wisdom continued to live and practise physic in London for nearly seventeen more years. In 1594 he took on an apprentice, a foundling boy now aged thirteen. It was a charitable deed, but also a sign of respectability; and yet he was still described, with telling ambiguity, as a physician and painter. We do not know how old he was when he died in late September or early October 1599, but he cannot have been far short of his eightieth birthday—a good age in any century, and perhaps testament to his skill as a physician. In his will, which (as was common) he drew up on his deathbed, he described himself as 'Gregory Wisdom of London, practitioner of physic, weak in body but of good and perfect mind and memory'. It is a businesslike document, as most wills are, but contains one or two peculiarities. He made bequests to a niece, a great-niece, and three great-nephews, mostly (tantalizingly, but this was not unusual) in the form of gold rings. He no longer seems to have had any closer family. We know that he had once been married, but his wife was presumably now dead. If he had had any children, he had either outlived them or become estranged from them. His own brother and sister were apparently dead too. Perhaps the hard, plague-struck 1590s had taken their toll.

Instead, most of his property went out of the family. 'My ancient and trusty servant', Joseph Buck, inherited the lease

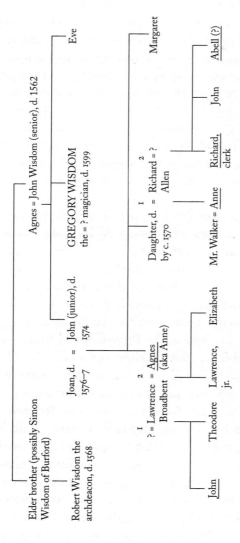

6. Family tree of the Wisdom family. Those members of the family to whom Gregory Wisdom left rings in his will are underlined.

to the tenement in the Savoy where Gregory had spent the last years of his life, along with a bequest of £10. He named three friends as his executors—a baker, a clothworker, and a doctor of divinity—and left the residue of his estate to be divided between them. He did not expect there would be very much to divide. One of the witnesses to the will was Richard Gyle: perhaps the man of the same name (or his son) who had fought, and won, the first court case against the Royal College of Physicians under the Quacks' Charter in 1545. As an old man, Gregory may have found his old allies more congenial than a family in which no one of his own generation still survived.

The professional record of Gregory Wisdom's life, then, suggests a self-made man who ploughed his own furrow, who was familiar with the seamier side of London life, and who was periodically in conflict with the establishment. This is not, however, the same thing as being a con-man, sorcerer, or would-be murderer. The only hint of a darker side to this man in the principal records of the Tudor state is a gnomic reference in the minutes of the Privy Council from May 1553. Like late 1546, this was a tense time: the young King Edward VI was dying, and he and his ministers were making a vain attempt to change the succession in favour of his cousin, Jane Grey. On 21 May, four men were arrested and placed in the Tower of London on suspicion of having said 'certain words touching the King's Majesty's person': they were to be kept incommunicado in order to prevent their concocting a common story for their interrogators. Almost as an afterthought, the same minute notes that 'for the same matter', Gregory Wisdom was placed in the Fleet Prison—Henry, Lord Neville's old haunt, and a less secure prison than the Tower. We can only guess at what these conspirators might have been up to. The records tell us nothing more, not even when and how they were released. If there was a plot, however, it seems that Gregory Wisdom was at least a peripheral part of it.

How, then, can we be sure that this eccentric, gifted, and underqualified physician was also our sorcerer and magician? Through several other documents which connect him to magical, or criminal activities—or both.

There is clear evidence that the Wisdoms had at least an academic interest in magic and the occult. In 1555, we find a 'Mr. Wisdom'—it could be the father or the son—petitioning the governors of St Bartholomew's Hospital in London; he wanted to have a book called 'a course upon the astronomy' which the hospital had inherited as part of the estate of a recently dead priest. *Astronomy*, as almost always in this period, meant the practical and occult art of astrology, not the dull and fruitless practice of mere stargazing.

The value they placed on occult books is made even clearer in John Wisdom's will of 1559. The bulk of his property he bequeathed to his wife, Agnes, with instructions that it was to pass to his three children on her death. In the meantime, each child received a token bequest. His eldest son, John (another painter-stainer), and his daughter, Eve, each received a ring.

Gregory, the younger son, was different. He and his father had shared professional interests. While John had given routine medical textbooks to his servant, he left two rather more arcane books to son. The first was 'the Lily of Medicine, in English': to give it its proper title, *Practica dicta lilium medicinae* by the early fourteenth-century French medical philosopher Bernard de Gordonio. It was a medical textbook, but a rather old and unusual one. Alongside much routine medical advice, it included a good deal of material on astrology (Gordonio was something of an expert on the subject) and on matters such as healing diseases caused by malevolent magic. It also had a good deal to say on what it called diseases of the imagination: in particular on that medieval preoccupation, lovesickness. Lovesickness was not, for Gordonio, a metaphor. He argued that sexual abstinence combined with temptation could cause gonorrhoea, and that intercourse was the cure. In the face of the new syphilis epidemic, and the hideous treatments which came with it, Gordonio's ideas would probably seem as attractive as they were dangerous. (Before he is dismissed entirely, however, it should be noted that Gordonio may have been the very first physician to take eyeglasses seriously.) If the book would have been useful to the Wisdoms, it is also clear why it was valuable enough to specify by name in the will: it was probably a unique copy. Gordonio's book was well known in England and its Latin text was widely circulated in print and in manuscript, but this is the only known reference to an English translation. John Wisdom must have owned a handwritten translation, since lost. It is another mark of the Wisdoms' self-taught status. Clearly they, unlike 'real' physicians, did not have much Latin.

The second book which John Wisdom willed to his son is more mysterious: a 'book in English called the Practice of Damell'. Again this is likely a handwritten book, as no printed book with a title remotely like that survives. However, one surviving English manuscript book is a close, if not an exact fit. Amongst the British Library's Sloane Manuscripts is a volume of magical texts, one of which begins with the words: 'Here beginneth the book which is called the Dannel.' We cannot be sure that this is the same text, but it is a strong candidate. The scribe who copied out Wisdom's will could, when faced with an unfamiliar word, easily have mistranscribed *nn* as *m*; and while the text in the British

Library does not use the word 'practice', it is a resolutely practical text, and, like other magical books, refers to the procedures it describes as 'experiments'. The identification is tempting because, as we shall see in Chapter 4, the magic which the *Dannel* describes is very similar to Wisdom's own. Although it is unlikely that the actual copy now in the British Library belonged to the Wisdoms, it is very plausible that they owned another copy, perhaps a variant version, of this text. This is a glimpse into the hidden world of magical texts, books which we know circulated surreptitiously in a slow-moving game of Chinese whispers, no two copies ever quite the same, the texts evolving as they passed from one hand to another. And it helps to make it clear that Gregory inherited his hobby as well as his profession from his father.

More damning evidence of Gregory Wisdom's interest in magic and fraud comes from two court cases in which Gregory became involved during the 1540s. The earlier and lesser of these dates from 1541–2, and its importance in the puzzle will only become clear later on. Since this case predates the Wisdoms' royal licence to practise physic, Gregory is described merely as a painter and a citizen of London. It is also clear that he was then making at least part of his living from dealing in expensive fabrics such as silks and velvets. It was fabrics of this kind with which he decked Lord Henry's chamber in 1544, in order to conjure Orpheus; he was, it seems, a man with an eye for such things. This particular court case turned on a shipment of silk and velvet, valued at £5, which a merchant named John Bendyshe delivered to Wisdom on 13 June 1541. The shipment was delivered on credit, with the understanding that Wisdom was to pay by 1 November. When no payment had been received by 21 November, Bendyshe sued Wisdom in the mayoral court.

However, Wisdom claimed that he had repeatedly tried to pay Bendyshe, who had refused to accept it, on the grounds that the true value of the goods was £6, not £5. Wisdom was indignant: the lawsuit was malicious, intended to 'vex and trouble' him, and carried out 'for love of the said velvet and other silks', which in any case 'were defective and not merchantable' when he received them. The resolution of the case is unknown, but it establishes that Wisdom had what was at least a sideline in fine textiles—and that he could be a difficult man to do business with.

This sets the scene for a murkier case which followed some three years later. On 27 November 1544 depositions were sworn at Westminster before the Court of Requests, one of the quicker and cheaper courts in England's confused and overlapping set of legal systems. Sir Nicholas Wentworth, a Buckinghamshire gentleman, was suing Gregory Wisdom over an expensive coat which, he claimed, Wisdom had stolen. As is usual with the Court of Requests, no final verdict survives, and so all we have are competing versions of events put by the two parties and the witnesses who testified for them. However, much of what happened can be reconstructed easily enough, and the case turns out to be about rather more than just a coat.

The agreed facts of the case are these. By late 1543, Gregory Wisdom was a known and trusted employee of the Wentworth family. In particular, this dealer in fine cloths had been entrusted by them with a valuable item: a coat made from crimson silk which was richly embroidered all over with pure silver. This gorgeous and extravagant item of clothing was agreed by all the parties to be worth at least £8— two or three years' wages for a common labourer. Wisdom had been asked to keep it in his London house for the use of Wentworth's son. Presumably such a courtly and fragile garment would only ever be used in London, and Wentworth did not want to subject it to the wear and tear, and the risk of theft, which hauling it to and from the family's country seat would have entailed. What is not clear is how Wisdom came to be taken into the family's confidences, so that it was he who was 'put specially in trust before all other to keep the said coat'. However, Wentworth did make it clear that he knew Wisdom to be skilled both as a physician and as an astrologer. It was presumably through services of these kinds that he had won the family's trust. It is this confirmation that Gregory Wisdom had magical interests (as well as a habit of acquiring expensive and impractical clothing) which makes it certain that this was the same man who defrauded Henry, Lord Neville. It also suggests that Wentworth was unwise to have trusted him.

At some point in November or December 1543, Wisdom left the precious coat in his wife's safekeeping at their London house. (This case provides the only evidence that there was a Mrs Wisdom: her name, frustratingly, is nowhere recorded.) He then travelled to Lillingstone Lovell, the Wentworths' seat—technically a part of Oxfordshire, although located deep within Buckinghamshire. Wisdom was travelling light, and indeed described himself as 'being from home and destitute'. Perhaps he had fallen out with another client. Whatever the reason, he did not even have a change of shirt with him. He was allowed, however, to treat the Wentworths' house as his own: he was even lent a silk shirt while his own was laundered. And, somehow, he wound up with 'certain pieces of gold' belonging to Sir Nicholas in his possession. After a short time at the Wentworths', he left in some haste—because of 'business', he said—heading for the Bedfordshire household of another wealthy client, Lady Elisabeth Radcliffe, with whom he planned to stay for some time. He departed wearing

Sir Nicholas Wentworth's fine silk shirt, carrying Sir Nicholas Wentworth's gold in his purse, and (according to one document) riding Sir Nicholas Wentworth's horse. Unsurprisingly, Sir Nicholas sent a servant to pursue him, a man named John Bradley.

When Bradley caught up with Wisdom, Wisdom explained to him, as he explained again to the court, that his having so much of Sir Nicholas' property was quite innocent. His own shirt was not yet dry, so he had kept the borrowed shirt on his back, 'and that with the said Sir Nicholas' love'. As for the money, Sir Nicholas had entrusted it to Wisdom for temporary safekeeping—he did not explain why Sir Nicholas should have done such a thing—and Wisdom had simply forgotten about it in his haste, since he was 'a man unaccustomed to be any man's pursebearer before'. Sir Nicholas, by contrast, alleged that Wisdom had planned to 'defraud' him of both. (There is no record of what happened to the horse.) This was not the main issue, however. Everyone agreed that the purse was returned to Bradley there and then, and that the shirt, too, was sent back in due course. They disagreed about what else was said between Wisdom and Bradley on the road. This was the crux of the case, and it is here that we return to the crimson silk and silver coat.

According to Wisdom's account, Bradley had a message for him. Sir Nicholas wanted the coat back, was sending messengers to Mrs Wisdom to claim it, and he wanted Wisdom to write to his wife, warning her to expect them. And Wisdom claimed that he did just that. But both Bradley and Sir Nicholas denied that any such exchange had taken place. Sir Nicholas, by his own account, only began to worry about the coat some time after Wisdom's hurried departure. He feared, perhaps after the close call with the shirt and purse, that Gregory and his wife might 'defraud' or 'beguile' him of the coat too. Sir Nicholas claimed that this was why, in January 1544, he sent two servants to the Wisdoms' London house: the same man, John Bradley, accompanied by one Richard Woode, a tailor and a tenant of the Wentworths from Marylebone. The dispute between Wisdom and Wentworth turned on rival accounts of this visit.

The accounts which Bradley and Woode gave to the court were clear and almost identical—perhaps suspiciously so. They had arrived on Thursday 31 January to find that Gregory Wisdom was not at home. His wife was there, however, with a maidservant. They introduced themselves and asked to see the precious coat. Mrs Wisdom brought it to them, and delicately unwrapped it from the trussed sheet in which it was stored. Bradley was impressed by it, declaring that 'this coat will be fit for my young master'. Mrs Wisdom showed herself concerned for the coat's safekeeping, urging the visitors only to rest it on its sheet, so as to prevent the silver from being rubbed. Once they had examined it, she carefully packed it away again, and they asked her to keep it until one of them came to collect it. Their reasons for the visit, they told the court, were threefold. First, to establish that the coat was still safe. Second, to charge the Wisdoms strictly that they should not hand the coat over to anyone claiming to be visiting on Sir Nicholas Wentworth's behalf, but only to Bradley or Woode themselves. Third, the visit allowed Bradley and Woode to inspect the coat, so that they could be not be fobbed off with a cheap imitation at a later date.

Their account, however, suggested that Mrs Wisdom was less interested in the coat than she was in a visit from men who had recently had some dealings with her husband. She had not, she said, heard from Gregory for some time. She did, however, have a shrewd idea of where he was likely to be, for as they were preparing to leave, she stopped them

and asked them if they might be able to pass a letter to the
servants of Sir Humphrey Radcliffe or of Mr Harvey. When
Wisdom had left the Wentworths', he indeed had gone to
the Bedfordshire estate of Edmund Harvey, to visit Harvey's
daughter, Lady Elisabeth Radcliffe—Sir Humphrey's wife.
Both Bradley and Woode testified that Mrs Wisdom was
agitated by this, 'weeping and saying that her husband used
her unkindly to be so long from her, sending her no word'. She
said that Gregory's treatment of her was enough to 'make her
a miswoman': a striking phrase which both men remembered
her using. A *miswoman* was a euphemism for a prostitute:
Mrs Wisdom was fearing, or threatening, that she would be
forced onto the streets while her husband toured the country
households of aristocratic ladies.

By contrast, Gregory Wisdom's own account to the court
of Bradley and Woode's visit did not mention his wife's
unhappiness, but it did add one crucial detail. After the coat
had been wrapped up again, Wisdom alleged, Bradley asked
Mrs Wisdom to hand it over. Since, in this version of events,
she had already received a letter from her husband informing
her that this was planned, she did as she was asked. Bradley
then gave the coat to Woode, who 'immediately closed the
said truss with the coat under his gown' and left with it. Sir
Nicholas, of course, denied that any of this had happened. In
due course, he asked the Wisdoms to return the coat, and
they protested that it had already been handed over. After
repeated requests, by the end of the year Sir Nicholas started
legal proceedings.

What really happened? We cannot be certain on the basis
of the evidence surviving, but Wisdom's track record makes
it fair to suspect that he was the guilty party. His account
of the conversation on the road is not wholly plausible, and
his contacts in the textile trade mean that he would certainly

have known how to dispose of the coat for a good price. A few curious features about this case are worth noticing, however. Wisdom's allegation—that Sir Nicholas had, in fact, been swindled by his own servants—was a clever one, and it was set up in such a way that it was difficult to disprove. Moreover, he claimed some corroborating evidence for this, from an intriguing source. As the argument over the coat bounced back and forth, Wisdom claimed that he had, at one stage, discussed the matter with Sir Nicholas' wife. Lady Wentworth had tried to avoid taking sides, saying, 'It were sin, Master Wisdom, to belie either Bradley or you.' This in itself is striking—that she should have refused to support her husband in his suspicions, instead treating Wisdom and Bradley as equally credible. But there was more. 'As far as I can remember,' she added, 'Bradley said that the coat was at Woode's house.' And Wisdom also claimed, tenuously, that the Wentworths' horsekeeper had said that Lady Wentworth had told him too that Woode had the coat.

Of course, neither Lady Wentworth nor the horsekeeper could be witnesses in Wisdom's favour, but Sir Nicholas did not attempt to rebut these claims. As well as muddying the water, this evidence suggests that Wisdom had a rather closer relationship with Lady Wentworth than he did with her husband. It was a well-established cliché that gentlemen might be cuckolded by their wives' physicians (men, after all, who might not only be left alone with women, but might legitimately touch or undress them). Whether that was the case here, we cannot tell. But it may be relevant that when Wisdom left the Wentworths', he did so in order to visit another aristocratic lady whose husband was not with her, and that his own wife was so unhappy about his prolonged absences. Perhaps, then, Sir Nicholas suspected that he had been 'defrauded and beguiled' of more than a coat.

In any case, Sir Nicholas clearly now believed that Wisdom had entered his service on false pretences. He claimed to have discovered that Wisdom was 'better studied in astronomy than in physic'—*astronomy* again meaning astrology. Wisdom's interests in medicine, Wentworth now believed, were a cover for his magical studies. And indeed, Wentworth claimed to have been 'defrauded by his science of astronomy and other craft'. Exactly how Wisdom's magical learning helped him to trick the Wentworths out of their property is unclear, although there are some obvious possibilities. Wisdom's skill as an astrologer had perhaps won Lady Wentworth's trust, or even her affections. Wisdom had no doubt originally offered his own services to care for the coat itself; indeed, given his taste for and expertise in impractical silken clothes, he most likely arranged for it to be made in the first place. Perhaps, as a dutiful astrologer, he warned that there was a risk of the coat being stolen if it were not carefully protected—a warning which he would have been able to cite, sorrowfully, as proof of his own skill once the theft had taken place.

So we now know where Wisdom was spending his time during those long weeks in November and December 1544, when he was resident at the Neville household in London and Lord Henry was concerned that his magical ring was slow in coming. This was precisely when the Wentworth case was being heard before the Court of Requests. As Wisdom was trying to fend off the legal consequences of one fraud he had perpetrated against the aristocracy, he was busy setting up another, even more ambitious scheme. And these, of course, are only the schemes which reached the law courts. We do not know what it cost Lady Radcliffe to have

Gregory Wisdom as a houseguest for a month or more, but we can be sure it was more than his board and lodging, and probably more than a silk shirt. Nor can we know how many other nobles and gentry fell for the patter of this plausible, ambitious swindler with an eye for the finer things of life. What we can do is look more deeply into the worlds of magic and criminality in which he dealt.

3

The Underworld

Henry, Lord Neville, does not seem to have been a bookish young man. That was unlucky, because during the same winter that he was being defrauded and bamboozled by Gregory Wisdom, a book was published which could have solved his gambling problems more effectively than any magician. It was the first of a series of books and pamphlets written over the next fifty or more years which offer a glimpse into London's criminal underworld, and to how it went about parting fools from their money. The book, apparently the work of one Gilbert Walker, was called *A manifest detection of the most vyle and detestable vse of Diceplay*. It is as instructive to us as it would have been to Lord Henry, for it provides a unique glimpse into another of the worlds where Gregory Wisdom lived and worked: the networks of fraud and crime which pervaded Tudor London.

The book is a staged dialogue between two characters. It was a common enough literary device, and Walker did not even give them names: they are merely 'R' and 'M', anonymous everymen. 'R', we are told, is a 'raw courtier, as one that came from school not many months afore'—a man much like Lord Henry, albeit of lowlier birth. 'M' is a more worldly wise acquaintance. 'R' opens the book by explaining, perplexedly, how his fortunes had taken an unexpected turn for the worse. His story began, as many London stories did, in the nave of St Paul's Cathedral: not the silent stonework of Wren's

¶ A manifest de-

tection of the moste vyle and detestable
vse of Diceplay, and other practises lyke
the same, a Myrrour very necessary for
all yonge Gentilmen & others soden-
ly enabled by worldly abūdace,
to loke in. Newly set forth
for their behoufe.

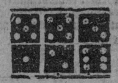

¶ Democritus.

Si te ris vous estes plus solz que ne ries
 de me veoir rire
De vous et de voz actes sont plus que mon
 rire plut dire
Tant ilya a vous redire et aulx plus sages
 de vous tous.
Qui est pleine fol qui ne rit de vous.

¶ Fortune vient a point.

---

7. Gilbert Walker, *A manifest detection of the moste vyle and detestable vse of Diceplay* (*c.*1555), title page. A first edition published in 1544–5 no longer survives.

cathedral, but the wooden-roofed structure that was destroyed by fire in 1666. Old St Paul's was more than the seat of the Bishop of London. It was London's most important public space, and God's service was only one of its uses. The cathedral's enormous nave was a place for business, for assignations, for friends to meet, for enemies to negotiate, for pickpocketry and pimping, and for innocents to be snared and sucked dry. In 1561 Bishop Pilkington lamented how far Mammon had encroached on this particular house of God: the nave was used 'for all kind of bargains, meetings, brawlings, murders [and] conspiracies', the area around the font was where debts were settled, and the underground chapel was 'by report as fit a place to work a feat in' as a brothel—there is little doubt what kind of 'feat' he meant. All this was, he added, 'so well known to all men as the beggar knows his dish'; and indeed, St Paul's was thick with beggars of all kinds. Alongside the destitute were young men like 'R', the raw courtier: youngsters who had come to London to make their fortune, and who had come to St Paul's, the great bazaar and hiring place. It was a place to meet friends, to make new ones, and, if nothing else, to walk up and down sheltered from the cold and the rain.

But 'R' had struck lucky. 'As I roamed me in the church of Paul's', he had spied a gentleman walking there, 'dressed in silks, gold and jewels', attended by servants dressed in similar splendour. The two men caught one another's eyes, and while R was trying to work out how best to speak to someone whose status was so much higher than his own, the stranger spoke first. He had, he said, noticed R padding miserably around the cathedral for half an hour, 'with such heavy and uncheerful countenance as if you had some hammers working in your head'. He himself, he said, had come to meet a business partner who had failed to appear. So he suggested that they pass the time by making acquaintance; for, he said, R's face was familiar, but he could not immediately place it.

Grateful for any company, let alone such an illustrious personage, R fell to talking with the stranger, and said enough about himself to make his status clear. He was one of the hundreds of young hopefuls desperately clinging onto the bottom rung of the political ladder, struggling to climb, to put on a show of wealth beyond his means and of courtliness beyond his upbringing, and aware that London was a furnace which devoured country boys every day. The stranger showed understanding for R's precarious situation, praised him for his prudence, and offered to keep an eye on him, and 'now and then show you a lesson worth the learning'. In the meantime, he invited R to join him for what would be, he warned, only a homely and simple dinner. How could a young courtier refuse?

They went to the stranger's lodgings, where they met his wife—who gave R an honest and friendly welcome—and where R admired the elegant and quietly expensive furnishings. The contrast with his own digs—'somewhat loathsome, and pestered with company'—was uncomfortable. As dinner was served, a number of other gentlemen arrived to join the party, and the lunch passed in a head-turning whirl of partridge, quail, wine, and sophisticated conversation. The host himself made much of his own humble status, all the while dropping hints that he was on intimate terms with some of the greatest men in the land. This was, he implied, simply to be expected of any member of that company. R was starstruck.

'After the table was removed, in came one of the waiters with a fair silver bowl, full of dice and cards.' The host began the afternoon's gaming by throwing £20 of his own money into the pot to get the others started. R was hesitant, admitting he did not know the games they were setting to, but his

hostess offered to teach him a few simple dice games and he
could scarcely refuse. By the middle of the afternoon, he had
lost almost £2. Struggling to extract himself, he managed to
leave only by promising to join his newfound friends again for
supper, and leaving a ring in pledge of his return. And indeed,
he returned to the same house and company for two meals a
day every day for two weeks.

It slowly became clear that this was not simple hospitality,
and that the house's life revolved around the gambling tables.
Yet R remained convinced of his host's honour and goodwill.
Each player was asked, when he first drew a hand, to con-
tribute five shillings to the costs of the house, which seemed
fair enough for the lavish entertainment they received. And
R believed that he was beginning to understand the card and
dice games which were being played, partly because the host
had been playing alongside him and advising him. He had
been playing in this way for a week, he admitted, in which
time both he and the host had lost £40. It was a beggaring
sum for a young man such as this, but he was confident that
the loss was temporary. He had seen other players around the
table reverse losing streaks and make fortunes from nothing.
And in any case, he was confident of the company's honesty:
well-dressed, 'men of worship . . . such as, I dare say, would not
practise a point of legerdemain for an hundred pound'.

So much R, the young courtier, told his more experienced
friend M. M's view of the matter was rather darker. As soon
as R had met the stranger in the cathedral, he lamented,
'hooks were laid to pick your purse'. R had fallen into a well-
tuned criminal machine which would draw him in, gut and
fillet him, and spit out the remains when he had been picked
clean. It was the workings of this machine that, for the rest
of Walker's book, M proceeded to describe. It was the same
machine which was even then bleeding Lord Henry dry.

M's first and his main point was that London's criminals and fraudsters were more than solo pickpockets and opportunists. They worked on an organized and an ambitious scale, and had their own hierarchy paralleling, or parodying, the legitimate hierarchies of the secular world. As part of this, they had their own jargon—almost their own language: the coded slang which became known as the thieves' cant. The writers who described this underworld certainly made it seem more formal, more organized, and more invincible than was in fact the case. There seems to be at least a core of truth in the legend of the thieves' cant, however, because some cant words eventually made the transition into common English, and others remained part of criminal slang for centuries. For example, M explained that the thieves and tricksters used lawyers' jargon to describe their activities. This lent them a veneer of respectability and of mystery; it also served as a grim joke on the way lawyers could, quite legally, use their own professional cant to beggar their clients. Hence London fraudsters' favoured term for themselves: 'escheators', that is, those who conveyed goods from one person to another. M said that they habitually shortened this to coin a new word for themselves and their activities: 'cheaters'.

This streak of self-justification was characteristic of the cheaters, in M's view. He described how, having brought a young gentleman to the brink of ruin, the cheaters might decide to reveal their secrets to him and recruit him to join their number. They would begin such an approach by pointing out that 'no man is able to live [as] an honest man unless he have some privy way to help himself withal, more than the world is witness of.' Noblemen could not live merely on their rents. Lawyers could not prosper 'if their pleas were short, and all their judgements, justice and conscience'. Merchants who bought and sold honestly would soon founder (Gregory

Wisdom would surely have agreed). Everyone was doing it. To become a cheater was not to step beyond the bounds of society. It was merely to start playing the game, and, having been the prey for so long, to take a turn at being the predator.

Only then did the cheaters begin to reveal their secrets to the new recruit. Some of them were simple enough. Dice could be loaded, or made slightly off-square, so that they would consistently favour certain numbers. There were craftsmen who specialized in making precision instruments of this kind, some of them resident in London's prisons. A practiced cheater might hold several different pairs of dice in his sleeve and switch neatly from one to the next, so changing the odds and avoiding a suspiciously long run of particular numbers turning up. Likewise, cards could be marked, pinched, or pricked with pins, or they might stick to the dealer's fingers. A mirror could be placed behind the dupe—the 'cousin', in the cant—angled so that his cards were visible to the cheater. Or a woman might sit at the edge of the room, sewing in silence, not heard and scarcely seen: yet she could see the cousin's cards, and would signal to the cheater 'by the swift, or slow drawing [of] her needle'. Or again, there were accepted codes by which cheaters might communicate with each other across the gaming table while their 'cousin' was none the wiser. For example, if a cheater swore an oath by 'honesty', or by St Martin, he meant that the truth was the opposite of what he said. And of course, there was the dazzling spell of friendship, opulence, and glamour which was woven around young men such as R, which lured them in, kept them in, and persuaded them to speak well of their hosts even as they were being systematically stripped.

These were the basic tools of the cheater. However, some scams were more elaborate. For example, when the cousin had already fallen in with some of the cheaters, another cheater might join them, impersonating an obnoxious drunk unknown to the company, and boasting of his skill at cards. The other cheaters would then invite the cousin to join them in putting the loudmouthed newcomer to the test. The drunk would proceed to lose money to everyone with reckless speed, until the point when the cousin was lured to bet all he had. On that turn of the cards, of course, the drunk would win everything. The other cheaters would accuse him of sharp practice, and a staged fight would ensue. The 'drunk' would be smuggled out of the tavern under cover of the melee, and the cheaters would then return to curse their luck together with the cousin, before going to join their confederate and share the spoils.

Later authors proceeded to describe elaborations or variations on these schemes, some plausible, some less so. In the 1590s, we are told of a card trick in which the cheater first defrauds the 'cousin' in a simple game, but promptly confesses what he has done. He then teaches the 'cousin' how to mark cards so as to practise the fraud himself, before inviting him to join in swindling a third person. Inevitably, however, the newcomer is a part of the plot. When the 'cousin' becomes confident in his newfound skills and when 'the sweetness of the gain maketh him frolic', he bets all he has: the two accomplices then turn on him and leave him beggared and bewildered. Nor were country 'cousins' with no taste for gambling safe. Another range of supposed scams turned on pieces of jewellery that appeared far more valuable than they in fact were. In one variant, the trickster or 'ring-faller' would drop a worthless ring in the street, and when 'some man of the country' stooped to pick it up, the trickster would call, 'Half part!', claiming a share of finders' rights. At best, the countryman could then be persuaded to buy a half share of the ring for much more than it was worth; at worst, he could

be abandoned in a tavern after a long negotiation and left
with a substantial bar tab to settle. A third approach was for
one member of a gang to learn a few facts about a country
newcomer—name, home county, whose respect they valued.
Another member of the crew would then use this information
to claim to be an acquaintance and strike up a rapport with
a fellow-countryman in the big city. The trust so easily won
would soon prove costly enough: we read of a maidservant
befriended by a man claiming to be her long-lost cousin, with
the eventual result that her master's house was burgled and
she was whipped for her part in the affair.

Yet the cheaters also had resort to less subtle methods. One
of their supposed disciplines was the 'high law': this was,
simply, highway robbery. A cousin who was clever or lucky
enough to get the better of the cheaters across the gaming
table, or even one who escaped before the bottom of his
pocket had been fished out, was likely to be followed and to
meet his newfound friends again, in a dark corner, where they
would relieve him of whatever he had not yet handed over.

In Gilbert Walker's pamphlet, M left his young friend R
with a warning: 'the feat of losing is easily learned'. Henry,
Lord Neville may have been an adequately skilled dice player,
but London's gambling houses were not places where one
could expect to win, and even his friends may have had
ways of tilting the table towards them which were more
effective than a magic ring. Moreover, it seems very likely
that Gregory Wisdom himself had friends amongst the
cheaters. As a surgeon, he will have had contacts amongst
London's brothels; and his dealings in stolen and suspect
clothing will have brought him another set of shady contacts.
No doubt it was through such contacts that he met Ninian
Menville and realized the rich pickings which Lord Henry
offered. And perhaps there is more. When Lord Henry and

his new magic ring went out gambling on Christmas Day 1544 with his friends, and won £30, it may have been simple luck. But it is possible that Wisdom arranged it, in order to convince his gullible young victim that the ring was working and that he should gamble even greater sums.

Gilbert Walker's book was one of the first of what became a staple of Tudor publishing: the genre of popular print which historians know as 'rogue literature'. These cheerfully picaresque pamphlets wore a thin veneer of moral purpose, but were manifestly sold as entertainment. They were so heavily copied from one another that the contributions of the individual 'authors' are sometimes doubtful: each new pamphlet retold popular tales and urban myths. By the 1560s, and even more by the 1590s, these books had a place in English life comparable both to modern crime reporting and to modern crime fiction: they aimed to warn, to shock, and to entertain, and above all of course to sell.

Some of the stories were plausible enough, like Gilbert Walker's; some are so plainly told for entertainment that it seems petty to ask whether they are true. Shakespeare's acquaintance Robert Green, the scurrilous pamphleteer who in the 1590s almost turned this genre into open fiction, told and retold the tale of how an exceptionally talented cutpurse (or 'nip') asked a cutler to make a new knife for him, to very particular specifications. When the job was done the cutler, intrigued, asked what this unusual knife was for. The 'nip', proud of his art, told the truth: it was for cutting purses from the unwary. The cutler's conscience was untroubled by this, for he was more interested in his business than in the good of the commonwealth. Only later did he realize that, during their conversation, the 'nip' had used his new knife to take the cutler's own purse. It was a story with a pleasing moral twist, and it had a little of the thrill which is always found in stories of master criminals whose wit and skill makes them unbeatable. But like most such stories, it is hardly likely to be true.

From these sorts of stories—unlikely, but not impossible—the pamphleteers proceeded to pure fantasy. A regular theme was that the criminal underworld was a highly organized and structured society, with strict divisions and hierarchies mirroring those of the legitimate world. So Thomas Harman's 1566 tract *A Caveat for Common Cursitors* purported to give a detailed taxonomy of different kinds of criminal vagabonds, and claimed that they formed a parallel society with recognized leaders and lines of command. Green claimed that London's pickpockets were formed into a guild, in a kind of parody of the livery companies that controlled the City's legitimate trades: they had a regular meeting hall, elected wardens of their company, and maintained a common fund for mutual assistance. This was mere scaremongering, not so subtly laced with satire (were the legitimate livery companies any less harmful to the commonwealth than thieves?). Other kinds of fantasies could creep in, too. Harman described how vagabonds would gather in deserted barns every night to hold orgies, in which every man among them would lie with two women and might demand, as of right, any woman in the company. In such stories we are coming close to the prurient legends of the witches' sabbats, those imagined nocturnal gatherings of eye-popping sexual depravity—legends in which earnest moral disapproval often served as a cover for mere pornography.

Eventually this world of comic criminality became unmistakably literary territory, a part of a tradition stretching back to the perennially popular tales of Robin Hood. Two of the chief playwrights of the early seventeenth century,

Thomas Dekker and Thomas Middleton, wrote pamphlets in this genre. And their contemporary William Shakespeare drew on it as well. When he first introduced one of his most popular characters, Sir John Falstaff, in 1596–7, his audience would instantly have recognized the type. At the beginning of *Henry IV, Part I*, Prince Hal merrily derides Falstaff's dissolute life: interested in nothing but food and drink, 'leaping-houses', and 'a fair hot wench in flame-colour'd taffeta'. The indignant Falstaff replies that 'we who take purses' are professionals, merely of the night rather than of the day: 'squires of the night's body...gentlemen of the shade', and governed as strictly by their own rules as are any honest men. Theft, he insists, is his 'vocation'. He proceeds to fulfil his vocation by plotting to ambush and rob a band of pilgrims en route to Canterbury, whereupon Hal hatches a second plot to rob the robbers afterwards. It is a typical picture: thieves have their structures and dignities, yet the very nature of thievery mocks those structures. And no one would ever have taken it as a sober description of 1590s criminality.

Beyond these romantic portraits, however, we can glimpse something of the reality of the criminal underworlds in which Gregory Wisdom and Lord Henry were entangled. Part of that reality is as perennial as cards and dice themselves. The cardsharps whom Walker's pamphlet described in England are recognizably the same as their Italian counterparts whom Caravaggio painted fifty years later, working together to gull a young innocent.

And the tricks, lies, and slick self-justifications of the cheaters' trade have always been the same. Here is one self-proclaimed (and understandably anonymous) modern cheater justifying his practice on his website:

8. Caravaggio, *The Cardsharps*, c.1595.

I always assume others will try to cheat. Cards have acquired a certain reputation over the centuries and I believe that playing cards are cheating devices that are occasionally used to play a game on the square.... Nevertheless, I consider myself to be an ethical cheat.... Some bastards simply deserve to be cheated.... In my opinion, credit card companies, banks, insurance agencies, parking tickets, etc.... (not to mention casinos) are just forms of legalized thievery. And on top of it they are extremely unethical. So why shouldn't I have the right to consider myself an ethical cheat in this unjust world?

Gilbert Walker would recognize this cheater's arguments: first, that it is justified self-defence, and second, that the whole world has 'privy ways' to help itself. Everyone is doing it, and always has been.

But it is another matter to see beyond the eternal temptations which dice, cards, and greed offer, and to find out what was distinctive about the criminal underworlds of sixteenth-century London.

Historians have rightly been sceptical about the rogue pamphlets' fantasies, but we do not need to believe all their tall tales to accept that there really was organized crime in Tudor London. There was no Mafia—that would have to wait until the eighteenth century, when Jonathan Wild, the so-called 'thief-taker general', built a criminal empire which for a few years effectively took over the policing of the City. Nor, yet, was smuggling a significant racket. But there were, at the least, certain taverns where pickpockets were said to gather; and there are accounts of barns being used as safe-houses for cutpurses, fences, and thieves to meet. Some criminal specialisms also seem to have existed. Loaded dice and marked cards do indeed seem to have been made by particular craftsmen, as Walker claimed. Likewise, there was the occasional professional forger, who could provide all sorts of useful legal documents for the right price.

Nor was it only sensationalist pamphleteers who took organized crime seriously. A criminal-justice statute of 1566 worried that England's cutpurses 'do confeder together, making themselves as it were a Brotherhood or Fraternity of an Art'. This may only tell us that Parliament had been caught up in one of its periodic moral panics, but there is some more level-headed evidence too. In 1585, when a London sessions of inquiry was busily condemning and hanging horse-thieves and cutpurses, a remarkable piece of testimony 'tumbled out by the way'. They were told of a man named Wotton, who having failed in careers as a merchant and alehouse-keeper, had set up a safe-house for pickpockets. It seems that this was more than an ad hoc arrangement, for it included 'a schoolhouse set up to learn young boys to cut purses'. The teaching in this 'schoolhouse' centred on purses and pockets hung upon hooks, with a series of small bells stitched to the fabric. The boys' challenge was to lift coins from them so lightly that the bells remained silent. When the premises were raided, the magistrates also found a series of rhymes and slogans in the cant written on the tables.

We do not have to follow the scandalized magistrates in believing that this budding Fagin's operation was part of a vast criminal underworld. It is a one-off report, and Wotton's decision to set up an establishment like this in permanent premises was surely foolhardy. No doubt most crime, even in London, was fragmentary, disorganized, irrational, and opportunistic. But the fears which the rogue pamphlets were stirring up were not entirely groundless.

And indeed, that fear itself was an important fact. If nothing else, the rogue literature testifies that this was an age of public fear of crime, and especially of crime committed by vagrants and the destitute. As England's rapidly rising population pushed ever greater numbers of men and women onto the road, respectable society's attitude towards vagabonds shifted from pity towards fear. A consistent theme of the rogue literature is that beggars were liars: their injuries faked, their hard-luck stories false, their poverty merely for show, and their piety and obsequiousness a mask which concealed contempt for the public. Robert Copland's pamphlet *The Highway to the Spital-House* described a group of beggars appealing to passers-by in God's name until one innocent gave them a coin: then they cried, 'Many a knave have I called master for this. Let us go dine.' It was a popular message, especially in an age where beggars were so numerous that one could hardly relieve them all without joining their ranks. Respectable citizens had to defy old-fashioned moral obligations by walking past beggars every day. To be told that the beggars were false was a useful salve to the conscience.

And indeed, some uncomfortable truths stand out beneath the glamour of the rogue pamphlets. Another of the con-man's favourite pieces of self-exculpation, down to the present, is that it is impossible to con an honest man. This suggests that tricksters are a rough-edged part of a society's moral economy, allowing the greedy and vain to spear themselves on their own follies. But while the greedy and vain make easy targets, so do the simple and honest. Like all predators, sixteenth-century cheaters seem to have concentrated on the easiest as well as the fattest prey. An early seventeenth-century account describes a wealthy farmer who arrived in London suffering from corns. His landlady found a quack who proceeded to lame him. As a result, he was confined to his bed in agony for six months, the landlady acting as a virtual jailor and bleeding money from him for his upkeep and his dubious medical care. It was hardly an improving tale.

This nasty little scheme at least produced a good return, but a notable feature of many of these tales is how little sixteenth-century criminals thought was worth stealing. It is an index of the depths of Tudor poverty. A single good meal, or clothes drying on a hedge, were common targets. A. L. Beier, the author of one of the most level-headed modern studies of Tudor crime, concluded that Elizabethan thieves would steal 'anything that was not nailed down', from lanterns off doors to (in one case) a swarm of bees. The pamphleteer Robert Green described a complex scam in which a man claiming to be a sea captain's servant rents a room for his master, and eventually borrows a sheet and two pillowcases in order to help transport the captain's goods: the purpose of the whole elaborate affair being the theft of the bed linen. A less complex crime, and one which appeared in the courts as well as in the bookshops, was 'hooking' or 'angling': using a fishing rod or something like it to 'fish' blindly through open first-floor windows at night, to see what could be snagged. Bed sheets and blankets were the most likely prey.

Gregory Wisdom, of course, was not involved in such desperate or small-time scams. If nothing else, his involvement in the trade in expensive fabrics situates him in the more lucrative end of the business. As usual, there was less money to be made from actual thievery than from dealing in stolen goods, and the 'brokers' who did this were notorious. 'There can hardly be a craftier knave than a broker,' wrote Green, and in 1601 Parliament considered legislating against the practice. This was one of the few ways in which organized crime might reach beyond the metropolis. A related problem was horse-theft, because the goods were so easily transported across the country. Horses could also be disguised, and Green had a merry tale of a stolen horse, suitably painted, being sold back to its original owner. Legislation requiring that no horse be sold without a sworn testimonial as to its rightful ownership created a market for forgeries. The business was like that of selling stolen cars today. This, perhaps, is how Wisdom disposed of the horse which Sir Nicholas Wentworth claimed to have lent him.

More certainly, Wisdom had access to another weapon in the trickster's armoury: medicine. According to Robert Copland in the 1530s, this was a common basis for a scam—as well it might be, when the desperation of a patient and the rarefied nature of medical knowledge combined to give even the most honourable physician a great deal of power. Copland described how a trickster would dress up as a great courtier-physician, typically claiming to be Jewish—which, as Wisdom knew, immediately suggested esoteric knowledge. This man would then accost a likely looking passer-by, perhaps a woman with a child, and tell her that he could see that the child was in the early stages of a disease that would kill him within two or three days. Insisting that he normally only treated princes and courtiers, he would press a useless drug onto the alarmed woman, and refuse to take payment for it. Yet there was only one dose of the drug. The following day, another member of the same crew would accost the woman, claiming that he too could see that the child had but days to live. Now thoroughly frightened, she would ask this newcomer what to do. He would offer to come and live in her house and treat the child for free, but he regretfully would ask her to pay for the drugs, which were beyond his means. Taking her money, he would in due course arrive at the house with 'drugs that be not worth a turd', and secure a fortnight's board and lodging over and above his profit. If all went well, he would eventually leave showered in praise for saving the child's life.

This was another merry tale, but we have hard evidence of scams like this being practised, because the medical establishment, jealous of its privileges as always, went out of its way to uncover them. The Elizabethan surgeon John Hall wrote a detailed and circumstantial account of the medical fraudsters he had met when working in Maidstone in the 1550s. On his account, such men would drift into town periodically, rent a room above a tavern, and post up bills offering treatment for a range of painful, disgusting, or embarrassing conditions. Such men often went by several pseudonyms, and never stayed in the same place for very long. They would ape the techniques of conventional medicine, for example asking all patients to bring urine samples with them. One of Hall's quacks, perhaps lacking the stomach for his work, claimed to be able to diagnose a patient merely by weighing a sealed stone jar of urine in his hand. Another could diagnose simply by looking the patient in the face.

We might, charitably, think that these people were not all shysters and frauds, but real and deliberate medical fraud certainly existed. In 1553 Cesare Adelmari, an Italian physician living in London, was summoned urgently to treat another Italian expatriate. When he arrived, he was told it was too late: the patient had died. But when he was shown in, Adelmari quickly realized that the man was merely unconscious, and would in fact quickly recover. The opportunity was too good to miss. Adelmari asked the man's family to leave the room for a short while, promising 'that he would work and show unto them a miracle in raising and reviving' the supposed corpse to life. He was as good as his word, and all would have been well if he had been contented with praise. However, his bill seems to have been almost as startling as the patient's recovery. When the suspicious family sued, he admitted the deception.

These generalities aside, there are two particular facets of London's criminal underworld which touch on Gregory Wisdom's dealings with Henry, Lord Neville. First, the nexus of gambling and prostitution; second, fraudulent magic.

Lord Henry's woes began from his gambling debts, and seems that his intimacy with London's brothels, too, was one of the snares in which he became tangled. Wisdom used both those troubles to bleed the hapless young man all the more. They provided the pincer of his plot, in his promises to change Lord Henry's unsatisfying luck and to end his unsatisfying marriage. It was a pincer whose operation was well established. Organized crime always prospers in the grey area between legality and illegality, when semi-legitimate businesses can act as shopfronts for more blunt criminality. This was the situation of gambling and prostitution in Tudor London.

In theory, the Tudor state took a thoroughly dim view of gambling. In 1542 Parliament passed an Act for Debarring of Unlawful Games, one of a series of pieces of legislation which shared the same futile hope: if dicing, carding, bowling, tennis, shove-groat, and all other such 'crafty games and plays' could be suppressed, the population would be forced to pass their leisure with the sport of archery. The hope was that this would produce a generation of skilled bowmen who could recover England's lost martial glory. With gunpowder weapons becoming ubiquitous, these dreams of refighting the battle of Agincourt were becoming ever more fantastic, but the myth of archery was a powerful part of English national identity. Fretting about the decline of archery was a national pastime.

Fretting, however, was all that could be done. The 1542 Act prohibited keeping or attending gaming houses, and barred any gaming at all by the lower orders (except at Christmastime, and then only under gentry supervision). But the final clauses added exceptions which left it toothless: the rest of the Act notwithstanding, masters were now allowed to licence their servants to gamble, and those with some landed wealth were allowed to licence any gambling on their property. These clauses look as if they were amendments added to the original text in Parliament. They reveal the fundamental weakness of attempts to control gambling: the nobility and gentry deplored gambling amongst the lower orders, but they themselves enjoyed it too much to outlaw the practice in earnest. As one Protestant minister lamented in 1550, 'Dicing and carding are forbidden, but dicing and carding-houses are upholden. Some in their own houses, and in the king's majesty's court...give example to his subjects to break his statutes and laws.' Gambling was even openly permitted in the debtors' prisons. In 1576 Queen Elizabeth finally bowed to the inevitable, and decided to make money by licensing gaming houses rather than waste it trying to suppress them.

As a result, all that the respectable opponents of dicing could do was to denounce it. They did so at length, in books which we can be fairly sure no hardened gambler would ever bother to read. The themes of this literature are predictable enough. Some authors attempted learned discussions of who had first invented dice (the consensus was that it was the Devil); most thundered against the idleness, greed, jealousy, dishonesty, profanity, hatreds, and violence which clustered around gaming tables. Philosophers argued that gambling was simply a form of theft; politicians worried that it impoverished the commonwealth. Some admitted the legitimacy of a few games, but usually they recommended backgammon or (best of all) chess, which involved no element of chance. But unsurprisingly, London was not troubled by illicit chess dens.

The most subtle and moderate argument against dicing was put by the sly Elizabethan aphorist John Harington. Alongside the standard run of criticisms, and a rather over-clever argument that gambling broke no less than nine of the Ten Commandments, he had some more pragmatic points to make. Learning to become a 'cheater', he argued, was not only immoral but also stupid. The skill needed 'to slur a die surely, to stop a card cleanly, to lay a pack cunningly', was not easily acquired. He claimed to know a cheater who had spent 'a month's earnest study beating his brains' in order to master a particular card trick. And the rewards simply did not match the work. Yes, 'when some good gull comes out of the country', the cheaters might have a good day from him; but mostly their pickings were thin, and scarcely paid for the illusion of living in high style. If readers were determined to make their livings dishonestly, Harington recommended that they become pirates or robbers rather than gamblers, for a prosperous cheater was 'as rare as a black swan'. And he compared dicing houses to desert islands, grim places where the only source of sustenance was the occasional shipwreck of others' misfortune. No doubt this was partly true, and the economics of the cheating business were shaky. Crime, proverbially, does not always pay. But the proverb rarely deters optimistic criminals. There were potentially huge sums of money to be made out of gambling, and Harington himself admitted that London was awash with young men desperate to do just that.

The gaming business could also boost its cashflow by providing ancillary services. Prostitution and gambling had a symbiotic existence. It was proverbial that (as Henry, Lord Neville's experience suggests) they shared the same clients. Bishop Latimer warned darkly, 'where dicing is, there are other follies also'. Harington, having argued that gambling broke all of the Ten Commandments except the prohibition on adultery, added that 'I dare be sworn that he that breaks nine of them, keeps none of them'.

As Gilbert Walker had claimed, the two businesses were intertwined. If the cheaters discerned that their 'cousin' had a weakness for female company, they would resort to the branch of their trade they called the 'sacking law', and find 'a lewd, lecherous lady to keep him loving company'. She might gull him directly, by pressing him for jewellery and rich entertainment. More usefully, she might urge him to abandon any caution he showed at the gaming table, urging him to reckless betting by making it clear that she was attracted to courage, not cowardice. Or she might press him to follow her instincts in his betting: ' "ye know not," saith she, "what may be a woman's luck." ' If the 'cousin' should refuse such advice, she would promptly fall into a studied sulk, and he would find that winning back her favour would be more costly than merely placing a doomed bet. Behind the glamour, this was an ugly business. The women's genitals would commonly be treated with 'surfling-water', a noxious preparation that shrivelled and tightened the skin: it could be used to counterfeit that most valued of female virtues, virginity. All to maintain the illusion of respectability while a young nobleman's pocket was emptied.

Robert Green described a related gambit, for which he claimed the cant term was 'crossbiting'. This was a trick as old as the hills. The client believes he is simply buying a prostitute's services in the usual way. But once they are in whatever tawdry bed the woman is able to maintain, an outraged man bursts in on them. He claims to be her husband, or her brother, and is perhaps brandishing a dagger. The client, in a weak position both physically and morally, can be relied upon to pay up handsomely, both to escape with his skin intact and to avoid a public humiliation. Of course, the whole thing is pre-planned. The man would be the woman's pimp, or, quite possibly, truly her husband. It is not a subtle trick, but it is easy to image Lord Henry falling for it. Cruder still, but equally serviceable, was the practice of prostitutes' drugging their clients and then robbing them down to their hose.

It is in any case clear that prostitution in general and brothels in particular played a pivotal part in the economy of London's underworld. Like gambling, prostitution was frowned on in a good Christian kingdom such as England. Yet by long tradition it was licensed and tolerated, for a range of reasons, some more honourable than others. Necessity was one. Those territories which had attempted to stamp out prostitution entirely had found that it was remarkably difficult to do so.

There was a steady supply of, and a ferocious demand for prostitutes, especially in the cities and near armies. There was a case for keeping the trade where it could be seen and regulated. When Henry VIII invaded France in 1513, he tried to ban prostitutes from actually accompanying his army, but soldiers and sailors at home would not be gainsaid. Pressed men in the Navy were not allowed shore leave in London, lest they escape; but they were allowed to receive visitors on board ship while anchored in the Thames, and London's pimps and bawds ensured that they did so. It was an unappealing trade, but it is difficult to buck the market.

Prostitution was also understood to have a useful social role to play, as a safety valve. The sexual drive of young men was assumed to be almost irrepressible. The best solution to this was of course marriage, but this was not always practical. Apprentices were forbidden by the terms of their employment to marry, even if they could afford to do so. Soldiers and sailors might well be married, but their wives were a long way away. Allowing brothels to meet their needs was an unsavoury solution, but city fathers feared that the alternative was gangs of young men roaming the streets in search of female flesh, and that their own daughters might not be safe. As St Thomas Aquinas argued, sewers are unpleasant, but a city with no sewer is worse. Better to channel male sexuality into one place, towards women whose morals were assumed already to be destroyed, than to see it spill over to the ruin of innocent women.

For of course, this whole debate was underpinned by sexual double standards. Fornication was a sin for both sexes, but for men, especially wealthy men, it was a venial offence, indulged by society. For women, it was *the* sin, and even if it did not bring the inescapable shaming of pregnancy, it instantly attracted the label 'whore'. A 'whore', whether her services were for sale or not, was a symbol of corruption. She might be raped with impunity. Indeed, it was common enough for women to become prostitutes following a rape, or a gang-rape. In some parts of Europe, this seems to have served as local society's way of telling a woman that there was no other living left to her. In England, it was more common for country girls to be, in effect, sold to pimps or bawds for prostitution: they would be raped to ensure that there was no going back. Yet most commonly, women were drawn into prostitution 'voluntarily', out of immediate need. For many of them it was neither a long-term nor a full-time occupation, but it was one of very few ways a destitute woman might feed herself and her children. The grim moral–sexual economy of early modern England not only had a place for prostitutes: it both demanded and ensured a steady supply of them.

The third and least respectable reason for official toleration of brothels was that they made a great deal of money. London's principal brothels or 'stews' at Bankside in Southwark were officially licensed by the Bishop of Winchester, and they made a significant contribution to his income. It was undignified, but it was too lucrative to change.

There were a dozen or so brothels at Bankside, run both by men and by women, and dominated by a small clique: bawds and pimps seem to have moved regularly from one house to the next. However, the long medieval toleration of prostitution was coming under pressure in the sixteenth century. The syphilis epidemic led to panicky attempts to shut brothels across Europe, and there were periodic attempts to close down Bankside from 1506 onwards. Moreover, the Protestant Reformation brought with it a less flexible attitude to public morals. Many Protestants wished to see adultery made a capital crime for both men and women, and although

this grisly ambition was not fulfilled until the Civil War era
(and even then almost never acted on), it spoke of a reluctance
to tolerate moral evils whether they were a safety valve or
not. Henry VIII, a king whose reverence for the sacrament
of marriage only increased the more he himself celebrated it,
was affected by the new religion's moralizing tone, and drew
on its rhetoric when he closed the Bankside stews for the last
time in 1546.

As the medieval tradition should have warned him, the
effect of this was not to eliminate prostitution but to scat-
ter it. Three years later, Bishop Latimer lamented, 'How
God is dishonoured by whoredom in this city of London;
yea, the Bank, when it stood, was never so common!...It
is marvel that [London] doth not sink, and that the earth
gapeth not and swalloweth it up.' But the truth was that even
official toleration for prostitution in London was continuing.
Only months after the suppression of the Bankside stews,
a licence was granted for the yeoman of the royal bears 'to
bait and make pastime with your Grace's bears at the accustomed place at London, called the Stews, notwithstanding
the proclamation'—a sure sign that good pastime was still
being made in Southwark, whatever the King had ordered.
And those prostitutes who had been driven out of Southwark
did not travel far. Some went to what threatened to become
a new Bankside, the precincts of St Martin le Grand, within
the City itself and almost under the shadow of St Paul's. In
the 1570s, the Lord Mayor complained that he could hear
the bawdy revels from his own residence in the Guildhall.
But most, however, took refuge in the suburbs, which, like
Bankside itself, were beyond the immediate reach of the City
authorities. 'Suburb' became a code-word for vice, as it now is
for middle-class dreariness. When Shakespeare's Portia asked
her husband Brutus if she was merely a harlot dwelling 'in

the suburbs of your good pleasure', the audience would have understood just how barbed the taunt was.

As prostitution was driven to the fringes of toleration, it became enmeshed with Tudor society's other corruptions. This was the more so in a period when London's population and its economic polarization were both growing very rapidly. There were now more, smaller, and more informal brothels than before, and the link with gambling was all the closer. As one wit put it at the time, 'cheaters and bawds go together like washing and wringing'. It was a mutually advantageous arrangement. In the established brothels, pickpockets, thieves, and brokers would gather for business and for pleasure. Conversely, the gaming houses owned or exploited by the 'cheaters' provided an opportunity for 'pennyrent' prostitutes who lacked permanent premises to pick up business, and to pursue scams such as crossbiting. Prostitution was the hub around which all London's underworlds turned: gambling, fraud, and theft, but also, as we have seen, soldiers and sailors with their new and frightening diseases. They rubbed shoulders with young men from respectable or even noble families, in search of some excitement; and with the enterprising medics who were willing to exploit such unsavoury opportunities in whatever way they could.

Gregory Wisdom's business and his profession will have given him ample contacts with London's less respectable citizens, contacts that it seems likely he exploited. However, what we know is that he had his own particular specialism: the use of magic to defraud. From his first offer to make a magic ring for Lord Henry, through the schemes involving the conjuring of Orpheus and hidden treasure, to the final murder plot, the claim of magical powers was the centre of Wisdom's snares.

Magic and supernatural practices have long been used to concoct frauds on a heroic scale. It is, again, a timeless theme. Stories of how the prophet Daniel debunked the fake magicians of Babylon had can be found in the Greek text of the Old Testament, spurred on by Judaism's scorn towards those who worshipped images. A court in London in 2002 heard how a businessman and his wife were defrauded of £30,000 by a man claiming to have a potion from Cameroon which he could use to manufacture £50 notes. The logic of these scams is inexorable: if you are able to persuade someone that you have access to hidden powers or secret knowledge, they can often be persuaded to part with money, and the more spectacular the powers promise to be, the more money can be extorted.

The simplest form of magical scam, and the most commonly sold magical service, was divination: claiming to use magical means to tell clients' fortunes or answer their questions, in particular questions about lost or stolen property. This kind of common sense or fairground 'magic' perhaps scarcely qualified as fraud, trading as it manifestly did on the practitioner's shrewdness. Yet some debunkers certainly thought it worth denouncing. The popular fifteenth-century devotional text *Dives and Pauper* was damning about this kind of magic, and warned that the uncanny accuracy of the magicians' answers should not be taken at face value. If they hit on the truth, the book cautioned, it might be by luck, shrewd reasoning, or (a sign of the slipperiness of 'magic' as a concept) 'by book of prophecy'. But alternatively, readers were warned, magicians could often find stolen property because they themselves were thieves, and in league with others, 'as taverners, brewers, hostlers', ready to sell stolen goods back to their rightful owners.

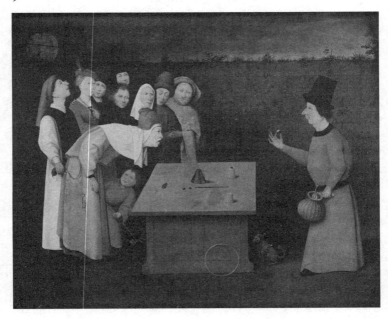

9. Hieronymous Bosch, *The Conjurer*, c.1475–80. Fairground conjurers like this were widely assumed to be frauds.

A more obviously lucrative branch of magic for fraudsters was alchemy, the art defined by its greedy customers (but not always by its learned practitioners) as that of transforming base substances into gold. Despite the Tudor period's open-mindedness towards magic in general, alchemists or 'multipliers' had already become bywords for fraud. When Ninian Menville introduced Wisdom to Lord Henry, he insisted that he was more than an 'unperfect multiplier'. They may have had in mind a character from that favourite of sixteenth-century readers, Chaucer's *Canterbury Tales*. In the *Canon's Yeoman's Tale*, an alchemist promises his credulous client that by heating mercury and charcoal in a crucible, and adding a secret powder, the mercury can be transmuted into silver. In fact, a piece of the charcoal had been hollowed out, and the hole filled with shards of silver and plugged with wax. When the fire had vaporized the mercury and burned the charcoal, the silver was revealed. The client, awestruck, paid £40 for a vial of the powder, which was in fact no more than crushed chalk and powdered glass.

A few years after Chaucer wrote, in 1403–4, a statute declared that none 'shall use to multiply Gold or Silver nor use the Craft of Multiplication', on pain of death. Yet as we shall see, the scientific claims of the more serious alchemists made a good deal of sense in contemporary terms. And for those who were willing to let their judgement be clouded by the prospect of limitless wealth, the possibility remained enticing. Ben Jonson provided a rollicking satire of this world in his 1610 play *The Alchemist*, in which a comic pair of fraudster-magicians set about gulling a swathe of fools (using the same trick as Chaucer had described, amongst many others). The play depended for its success on the audience's being willing to believe two things: first, that alchemy was likely to be a fraud, and second, that plenty of people might still fall for it.

Jonson's comic antiheroes, however, have more to their magical trickery than simple alchemy. They are enmeshed with the wider underworld—there is a strong suggestion that they are also involved with prostitution. And parts of their repertoire are strikingly reminiscent of Wisdom's dealings with Lord Henry. One of their clients is 'Dapper', who wants supernatural help with his gambling—in this case, not a ring, but a familiar spirit to advise him. They draw him in just as Lord Henry had been drawn in. They begin with a studied refusal to help him, on the grounds that what he is asking is both dangerous and illegal—the result being to ensnare him explicitly in the plot. (Indeed, Jonson's magicians even cite the draconian 1542 Act against Conjurations, which had been repealed a lifetime before.) Then come the promises of what the familiar will do for Dapper:

> He'll win up all the money i' the town ...
> And blow up gamester after gamester,
> As they do crackers in a puppet-play. ...
> Give you him all you play for; never set [i.e. bet against] him:
> For he will have it.

Hearing such delicious promises, Dapper becomes impatient, only to be told, as Lord Henry was, that he will have to wait. 'There must a world of ceremonies pass.' And when another client shows impatience with this kind of obfuscation, the magician uses a carefully calibrated burst of temper to restore control. As he helpfully explains in an aside:

> This will fetch 'em,
> And make 'em haste towards their gulling more.
> A man must deal like a rough nurse, and fright
> Those that are froward to an appetite.

If a client's credulity is to be kept simmering, the mixture of bullying, cajolery, mock-reluctance, and alluring but not outrageous promises needs to be kept steady. As Wisdom could have told us, executing complicated magical frauds is hard work.

This, then, was a specialized form of criminal trickery, with ambitions which went much further than those of the common cheater, ring-faller, or crossbiter. The trickster needed to invest time, effort, and (often) money in the business before securing any rewards. Such frauds might be built up over a long time, as Wisdom's were. In 1492, a London sorcerer named Richard Laukiston was arrested for defrauding Margaret Geffrey, a widow of the parish of St Bartholomew the Less. As a young, impoverished widow, with both a mother and her own children to support, her status was precarious: such women's roads might well end at Bankside. The obvious escape route was remarriage. Laukiston exploited this need. Explaining that it would be a good deed to help her remarry, he told her that his wife knew 'a cunning man, that by his cunning can cause a woman to have any man that she hath favour to'. If she was willing to invest only a little money up front, he promised, 'thou shalt have a man worth a thousand pounds'. It was a tempting prospect, but Geffrey initially refused. She did not have the cash to spend on such a project. Her only valuables, she said, were two bowls, apparently ornate ones, valued respectively at just over £3 and at ten shillings. Laukiston finally agreed to take these in lieu of cash payment. No husband materialized, of course, and eventually (in the legal terminology of the day) 'public infamy' led to their arrest. Both fraudster and victim were convicted of heresy and sorcery, but Laukiston was also required to repay Geffrey what he had stolen from her.

Such stories are rarely recorded before the end of the sixteenth century: the account of Wisdom's defrauding of Lord Henry is unparalleled in its detail. Only with the vogue for printed tales of roguery around the turn of the century do similarly detailed stories come to light, and as with all such tales, they need to be approached with caution. Two pamphlets in particular, though, give some further insights into the world of magical fraud and the ways in which it could be committed, by describing the activities of two notorious tricksters: Alice West and Judith Phelps.

Alice West and her husband John were from Fulham and, according to the pamphlet that described their activities for a sensation-hungry readership, they perpetrated a series of magical scams, some simple, some elaborate. At the root of them all was her claim to affinity with Titania and Oberon,

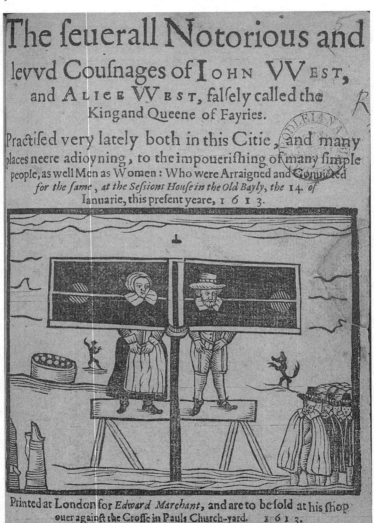

10. *The seuerall notorious and levvd cousnages of Iohn West, and Alice West* (1613), title page.

the Queen and King of the Fairies, whom Shakespeare had treated as fanciful but whom plenty of English people were willing to take seriously. Although fairy belief already had a nostalgic, old-fashioned feeling to it, magical handbooks from the later sixteenth century regularly enough included rites for summoning fairies, including the royal couple themselves. To early modern imaginations, fairies were not twee little Tinkerbells at the bottom of the garden, but anarchic, amoral, and whimsical spirits, fair-weather friends and dangerous enemies. Jonson's magicians had mocked those who believed in fairies, but Alice West's clients, at least, were willing to take them seriously.

For if any of the pamphlet's claims are true, West had a thriving little trade as a fraudulent fortune-teller, claiming that the fairies gave her knowledge of the future. It was good business: promising a gentleman that the wife he wished to be rid of would die soon, reassuring adulterous wives that their seafaring husbands would not return yet. One young man wished to know when his master would die, so that he could marry his mistress; she strung him along with promises 'till she had left his purse as barren as his brain'. She worked hard to make a good first impression on clients. We are told that she built 'a little Closet' in her house hidden by the front door, so that when callers came to have their fortunes told, someone would answer the door and take the clients' details while she listened, unseen. Then, when she met clients, they could marvel at the knowledge that the Queen of the Fairies had already given her.

At times the Queen of the Fairies did more than simply answer West's questions, and expressed her own preferences. Every so often, it appeared that Titania favoured a particular person, and West saw it as her duty to tell the lucky individual. One goldsmith's apprentice, who 'had the charge of more wealth than wit', was told that the Queen of the Fairies was in love with him. West told him to bring four silver-gilt servers to a prearranged place in the dead of night, and promised that they would be turned to gold and that 'there thou shalt confer with the amorous Queen of Fairies'. When he arrived, the would-be Bottom was instead ambushed by some hefty young men who relieved him of the valuables.

In another case, West told a rich gentlewoman that the Queen of Fairies wished to shower her with wealth. The lady was sceptical, but West asked her for a napkin and two shillings to provide proof. West then surreptitiously switched the coins for sovereigns, worth twenty times as much, before tying them up in the napkin. Speaking a few words over the parcel, she then promised the client that her first gift from Titania was ready; and the lady was duly amazed to discover it was true. West then urged her to put the two sovereigns in a safe, promising that if she opened it in a week, they would have doubled in value—and since West herself now guarded the key, it is no surprise that her prophecy was fulfilled. Several more such demonstrations followed, each one equally successful, until the moment when the lady, now convinced, was willing to leave a really substantial sum of money in the safe. She was promised that her £80 would become £1600; instead, it disappeared.

Much of this, the text implies, was good clean fun at the expense of the rich or stupid, but not all of her victims can be dismissed in this way. We are told that West promised 'a simple maid who had hoarded the best part of seven years' wages out of her good housewifery' that the Queen of Fairies favoured her. The hapless maid was persuaded 'to sit naked in a garden a whole cold frosty winter's night, with a pot of earth in her lap,' on the promise that Tita-nia would turn the earth into gold at dawn. West took the opportunity to steal the young woman's clothes along with her life savings—her only chance of marriage or of escape from servitude.

All of these tales were padding, however, for the principal story of West's villainy, for which she and her husband were in the end arrested. Some or all of the other tales may be apocryphal, but the main story is rather more circumstantial: we are told, in particular, the name of the victims, a Mr and Mrs Thomas Moore of Hammersmith. West insinuated herself into the Moores' confidences through their maidservant, who it seems—although the text does not say so—may have become an accomplice. In any case, she told the maidservant that the King and Queen of Fairies had appeared to her and told her that they wished to bestow 'great sums of gold' on the Moores. There were two conditions, she warned. First, the affair must be kept entirely secret, lest the fairies be angered and their gifts turned to curses. Second, the Moores must 'perform the due rites of sacrifice' first, rites that might require a little outlay.

The first of these rites, it turned out, was a substantial banquet for the royal fairies. How it was delivered we do not know, but it seems reasonable to guess that the Wests enjoyed it; they promised that the more that was spent on the banquet, the greater would be the reward. Second, a chamber had to be hung with the finest linens for the fairies' use. Wisdom had made similar preparations for the conjuring of Orpheus, and indeed it was a common trope. However, the Moores were wary of their promised good fortune, and the Wests went to some trouble to convince them. First, they laid on an elaborate tableau:

> They brought him into a vault, where they showed him two attired like the King and Queen of Fairies, and by them

little Elves and Goblins, and in the same place an infinite company of bags, and upon them written, this is for Thomas Moore, this is for his wife, but would not let him touch anything.

They were convinced for a while, but as his expenses mounted and the bags of gold remained in the realm of fairies, Moore's scepticism returned. He resolved to reveal the matter to a friend and ask for advice, and it is at this point that the account becomes more difficult for modern readers. We are told that Moore was struck lame before he could leave the house, and that Alice West promptly appeared to tell him that this injury was inflicted by the King of the Fairies, furious at Moore's intended treachery. But all was not lost. Titania had interceded with her husband and cooled his rage, and had given West an enchanted ointment to restore Moore's legs to full strength. Moore duly applied the ointment, and recovered his strength; and it 'gave no greater strength to his limbs then it did growth to his opinion'. The pamphlet's author thought that West's 'sorceries' were probably to blame for this incident; to modern eyes, it looks like suggestion, or—more likely— embellishment by the reporter.

In any case, West now had the newly convinced Moore buy chests, trunks, sacks, tubs, and barrels to be filled with the fairies' gold when it came. But as the chests remained unfilled, and Moore's worries began to rise again, the Wests mounted a last tableau, this time for the benefit of the maidservant. She was taken to a cellar and 'by some strong illusion' shown the royal fairies, together with treasure which she guessed came to £1700. We are told that she gave sworn testimony about this vision to the court which later tried the case, but it is likely that the Wests chose to work through her because she was corruptible, not because she was credulous. In any case, her report of this vision persuaded the Moores to hand over the sum of £80 which the Wests claimed was needed to complete the ceremonies. They took the money and fled, but were caught. Alice was whipped through the City and pilloried, and when the pamphlet was published in 1613, both were still in prison waiting to learn their final fate.

Compare these merry tales to the case of Judith Phelps, from nearly twenty years earlier. Phelps' character is similarly drawn: she was a cozening fortune-teller, married but operating independently from her husband. Much of her magical repertoire was similar, too. And again, the pamphlet which describes her career tacks a lesser and perhaps apocryphal story onto the main account. This second tale—which the author claims to be taking from Phelps' arraignment at the Old Bailey in 1594—is a variation on a now-familiar theme. It describes how Phelps, with two male accomplices, set out to defraud a wealthy widow living in the London parish of St Nicholas Shambles. The accomplices did some background research on the lady, and Phelps used the information to forge a letter of introduction, purporting to be from a friend of the widow's in the country. When admitted to the house, she read the widow's palm, 'discovering' in it various facts which her accomplices had already told her, and so impressing the lady further. Having won her confidence, the game could begin.

Still studying the lady's palm, Phelps asked if she sometimes heard 'a great rumbling when you are in bed'. Surprised, the widow said yes. This 'rumbling' was in fact the accomplices, who had been coming to beat on the front door in the dead of night, but Phelps' explanation was more alluring: 'your husband in his life hid about your house great store of treasure, for which cause there are spirits now that haunt your house.' She promised to find the treasure, but warned that the process might cost a little.

The ceremonies began: candlesticks were set in various parts of the house, and prayers were said. As part of this, Phelps had the widow put £100 of gold and silver in a purse, and wrap it up tightly in a thick ball of woollen yarn. However, Phelps prepared a matching ball of yarn, containing stones rather than coins, and managed to exchange them; then, pressing the now-worthless ball of yarn on the widow, urged her to 'lock this up very sure, and look not into it until I come again'. She explained that she had to consult a wise man who was acquainted with—again—the Queen of Fairies. In order to win this wise man's favour, she asked that the widow provide her with 'a fat Turkey, and a couple of Capons', so as to give him fit entertainment. Phelps then made her exit, with the money and with a substantial slap-up dinner for herself and her accomplices.

Her mistake was to go back for more. While she was away, the widow decided to check the ball of yarn, and discovering the switch, decided to trap her swindler. Phelps eventually returned and explained the next stage of the plan: the Queen of Fairies had instructed that twelve candlesticks be laid out around the house, with gold under each one. However, before this could be done the constable arrived and carried her off to Newgate gaol. She was duly sentenced to be whipped through the City.

Yet this story was simply a companion-piece to Phelps' more spectacular fraud, which was committed not in London but in Hampshire, where Phelps was practising as a cunning-woman. One of her neighbours in these parts was, we read, a 'wealthy churl' who was 'somewhat fantastical and given to believe every tale he heard'. So, having done her research in advance, Phelps hatched a bold plan to swindle him.

Seeing the man's wife outside the house one day, Phelps stopped as if thunderstruck and fixed the woman with an

unwavering stare. Understandably disconcerted, the lady of
the house asked this lowly stranger to explain herself. Phelps
replied:

> O mistress . . . you are the fortunatest woman I saw this many
> a day, for in your brows I see good fortune sit. Have you not
> a hollow holly tree standing near unto your house?

The bewildered lady confirmed that there was such a tree, and
Phelps asked, as a matter of urgency, to speak to her husband.
'If he be like you in the face, you will come to be exceeding
rich, for under that hollow tree there is great store of treasure
hid.' When she was brought before the husband, 'she likewise
looked him strangely in the face'. And as well as claiming to
read some few details about his life from his face (here her
advance research paid off), she confirmed that 'great sums of
gold and silver' were buried on his land.

They were eager to believe, but wanted proof. So she went
with them to the hollow holly tree and asked them to dig.
Within a few moments they found two coins: a sixpence,
and a gold angel, the latter worth ten shillings and a coin
often used in magic. Phelps had, of course, climbed into
their grounds and buried the coins there the night before.
Convinced, the couple agreed to employ Phelps' services to
find the rest of the treasure.

She named her fee at £14—which they jibbed at, but
accepted—and laid out the preparations which would be
needed. Many of these are now thoroughly familiar. 'Now,'
Phelps demanded, 'must I have the largest chamber in your
house behung with the finest linen you can get, so that nothing about your chamber but white linen cloth be seen. Then
must you set five candlesticks in five several places in your
Chamber, and under every candlestick you must put an angel
of gold.' But she also added a new twist. She had the master

of the house fetch a saddle and bridle, and led him and his
wife out into the yard:

> where she set the saddle on his back, and thereon girded it
> fast with two new saddle-girths, and also put a bridle upon
> his head. All which being done, she got upon his back in the
> saddle, and so rode him three times betwixt the chamber and
> the holly tree.

Following this bizarre and humiliating performance, she
instructed the two of them to prostrate themselves before
the holly tree for three hours, and not to move until she
returned: for she now needed to go to the ceremonial chamber
to summon the Queen of Fairies.

As they lay there, of course, she stripped the room of its
gold and fine cloths. But she apparently could not resist taunt-
ing her victims once more before she made her getaway. She
used some of the linens to swathe herself in white, wrapped
another around her head as a turban, and took one of the
candlesticks in her hand. So clad, she appeared in front of
her uncomfortable employers in the half-light as the Queen
of Fairies, and urged them to stay where they were a little
longer. Then she fled.

Finally, 'being half dead with cold', the 'churl' removed
his saddle and bridle, and stumbled back into the house, to
find Phelps and much of his property gone. And we read
that, berating himself for a fool, he rode into Winchester and
raised hue and cry after her. She was duly found on the road,
arrested, tried at the assizes 'and there received such deserved
punishment as the law would permit'.

It is difficult to know what, if anything, we can make of
stories such as these. It is certainly as well to be sceptical.

THE

Brideling, Sadling and Ryding, of

a rich Churle in Hampshire, by the subtill practise of one
Iudeth Philips, a professed cunning woman, or
Fortune teller.

VVith a true discourse of her vnwomanly vsing of a Trype wife, a widow,
lately dwelling on the back side of S.Nicholas shambles in London, whom she with her conferates, likewise cosoned:

For which fact, shee was at the Sessions house without New-gate arraigned,
where she confessed the same, and had iudgement for her offence,
to be whipped through the Citie, the 14.of February, 1594.

Printed at London by T. C. and are to be solde by
William Barley, at his shop in New-gate
Market, neare Christ-Church. 1 5 9 5.

11. *The Brideling, Sadling and Ryding, of a rich Churle in Hampshire, by the subtill practise of one Iudeth Philips* (1595), title page.

Wisdom's fleecing of Lord Henry is detailed in a confession by a victim who had no interest in embellishing the truth, while these accounts are taken from sensational pamphlets whose authors probably did not place any great value on accurate reporting. Many of the ancillary tales of Alice West and of Judith Phelps read as if they have grown in the telling; some are likely to be based on the work of other fraudsters, others are probably mere urban myths. The occasional implication that the women genuinely had some magical powers helps to make the stories even more slippery. Moreover, the satisfying moral shape of some (although not all) of these stories is suspicious. The tale of Phelps saddling and bridling the 'rich churl' particularly stretches credulity. It was a memorable enough image for the publisher to use it for his frontispiece, but it was more than mere surrealism. The image instantly evoked one of the best-loved medieval legends, of how the philosopher Aristotle—the embodiment of reason—was bewitched by the charms of Phyllis, the lover of his pupil Alexander the Great. She promised to quench his desire (as the medievals coyly put it) if she first allowed her to ride him like a horse. Phyllis riding Aristotle became a symbol of the inversion of all good order in society: reason submitting to passion, age submitting to youth, and man submitting to woman. It was a shocking symbol of the way God-given hierarchies were inverted by cozeners such as Phelps, and indeed by the whole deceitful, vice-ridden parody of good order which the rogue literature imagined the underworld to be.

And yet . . . if Wisdom's tale had been printed, we would dismiss it as incredible by these same criteria. If Phelps' riding of her 'churl' echoed the well-known story of Phyllis and Aristotle, perhaps that is what put the idea into her head. There are parallels enough between Wisdom's tale and the later ones to give them some credibility—the careful preparations and introductions, the chambers hung with fabrics, the promises of hidden treasure. And Wisdom's tale at least confirms that complex, lucrative magical scams could truly be planned and executed.

Ultimately, of course, we cannot know where the boundary or boundaries between truth and fiction lie in these stories, nor does it particularly matter. Even if West and Phelps never existed, the stories fastened onto them conjure them into significance. For these stories tell us what audiences at the end of the sixteenth century believed about magical fraud. They also tell us what they thought other English people could be persuaded to believe: buried treasure; multiplying gold; spirits, visions and prophecies; even the Queen of Fairies.

So where does this tour of the Tudor underworld leave us? It suggests a porous, interwoven, deceitful world, in which gambling, pickpocketry, highway robbery, prostitution, and the occasional complex, magical fraud all met. If Wisdom's case is a snapshot of this nexus of criminality, the other evidence we have seen corroborates and complements it. Despite the glamour and order which some of the Elizabethan writers gave to it, this was not an attractive world. It was a product of rapid population growth, especially in London; of a polarized economy, in which wealth was increasingly concentrated in the gentry, professional, and mercantile classes, while the majority struggled and a large minority had no reliable living whatsoever; and of a society which lacked the resources to police the morals it proclaimed. Perhaps this situation had become more acute by the 1590s—years of war, famine, and terrible social dislocation—than it had been in the 1540s; or perhaps it is simply better documented then. It would be nice to know what Gregory Wisdom, as an old man who had now attained some sort of piecemeal respectability, thought of the new fashion for rogue pamphlets which purported to describe the world he had once inhabited. Much of it must have seemed familiar.

But there is also more to this story than mere fraud and deceit. The victims of magical fraud could be taken in, not because they were exceptionally stupid, but because the lies which were spun to them were alarmingly plausible. To understand Wisdom's world, we need to understand the magic with which he deceived his victims, but in which he nevertheless believed himself.

4

The Magician

GREGORY Wisdom was, of course, a trickster, a liar, and a thief. He made much of his living by weaving illusions, the most lucrative of which was the illusion of magical power. All his dealings with Henry, Lord Neville were built around boasts that he could do things which in fact he could not do. And clearly, a great deal of this was deliberate fraud. But all?

The picture which Lord Henry painted from his prison cell was not one of a wholly cynical charlatan. The final episode, of the attempted murder, only makes sense if Wisdom had believed he might actually be able to do it. Only if the old earl had died would he have been able to lay his hands on a really substantial slice of the Neville family fortune, and there is no sign that he was offered any cash up front. Or again, there is the elaborate sumptuousness of the paraphernalia which Wisdom prepared for the conjuring of Orpheus, and which cannot have cost him much less than the £4 he claimed. Possibly he hired or borrowed it, but more likely he kept it—material which was useless in ordinary life, but which was invaluable for the costly, capital-intensive business of ceremonial magic. Or indeed, there is the magical ring with which the whole game began. Obviously, anyone certain that such a ring would work would use it himself, rather than selling it. But anyone certain that it would *not* work would not, as Wisdom did, ask to be paid by an annual pension rather than in a lump sum. His willingness to trust in his patron's continued good will and a paper promise suggests some optimism that there would be winnings to share.

Wisdom was obviously taking a gullible young nobleman to the cleaners. But this does not mean that he regarded the whole magic business as entirely phoney; more likely, he hoped that he might be able to do some of what he claimed. Perhaps he preferred to test his magic ring's effectiveness on Lord Henry's purse rather than his own, but his behaviour makes little sense unless he thought it was at least worth testing. Rather than a mere fraud, he appears more like a researcher lying optimistically about his results in order to secure the next round of funding. As the literary scholar F. H. Mares said of the antihero of Jonson's *The Alchemist*, Wisdom is like 'a man who takes to crime to keep himself going while he perfects his infallible system for winning at horse-racing, or poker-machines, or who misappropriates other people's money to finance his own speculation on the stock-exchange'. It seems likely that he had spun himself as well as his victim into his deceits. But then they were both caught in a much wider web of magical hopes, dreams, ambitions, and terribly plausible theories. It is time to explore that web, and to see how tightly Gregory Wisdom's practice of magic was woven into it.

Magic is almost impossible to define, but most of us have the sense that we know it when we see it. One approach is to define it by contrast with what we nowadays call science: magic is technology that does not work. But as we shall see, this boundary turns out to be alarmingly porous. Neither Tudor magic nor Tudor science (such as it was) respected it. Another approach contrasts magic with religion: magic tries to manipulate supernatural powers to achieve mundane, worldly ends, while religion humbly submits to supernatural powers in pursuit of higher ends. But in practice magic was not always so selfish or so mechanistic, and religion not always so humble or so high-minded. Or perhaps magic is a matter of status: it is a name for religious or scientific practices which are illegal, socially unacceptable, or widely despised. But that threatens to collapse science, religion, and magic together into a relativistic mush in which all three lose their distinctive flavour. Moreover, it misses one of the most remarkable features of magic in the Renaissance: that it was a matter which concerned not only pennyrent conjurers, but also some of the finest minds of the age. And here we need to pay a short visit to the great magi of the Renaissance.

The Renaissance was a mood of restless questioning which intoxicated Italy in the fifteenth century and the rest of Europe in the sixteenth, and it was fuelled by one ambition above all: to rediscover the wisdom of the ancient world, those forgotten glories which certainly (who could doubt it?) outshone anything in the more recent past. Ancient texts became talismans. Politics rediscovered Cicero; theology rediscovered the Bible in its original languages. But not all of the rediscoveries were so straightforward. Amongst them was the *Corpus Hermeticum*, a text of magical ideas strongly informed by Neoplatonic philosophy. In reality, it dates from the second or third centuries AD. However, its mid-fifteenth-century discoverer, Marsilio Ficino, believed the claim that the *Corpus* makes for itself: that it (with another, even more magical text) was the work of Hermes Trismegistus, 'Thrice-Great Hermes'. This name actually refers to the Egyptian deity Thoth, the scribe of the gods, but Ficino and others took it to be the name of a surpassingly ancient Egyptian priest, custodian of a pristine theology which predated Moses. On this reading,

the *Corpus* was written in something like the fifteenth century
BC. Since precedence determined authority in the Renaissance
mind, Hermes Trismegistus had suddenly jumped to the head
of the line.

What Ficino actually did with the Hermetic writings was
fairly tame. The 'magic' he recommended was mystical and
philosophical in nature, and centred around drawing the
astrological influences of the planets down to earth in particular times and places. Ficino was mainly interested in this
as a medical technique. A new dimension was added by his
younger and more provocative contemporary, Giovanni Pico
della Mirandola, who blended Ficino's Hermetic magic with
another fake relic of the ancient world: the set of Jewish
texts known as the Kabbalah. This mystical tradition first
came to Christian Europe's attention in the thirteenth century, and it has maintained a steady following pretty much
ever since. At its heart is an improbable belief which might
have been tailor-made to appeal to Renaissance dreamers:
that the Torah, the first five books of the Hebrew Bible, contains a series of elaborate codes, hidden in the text by Moses
himself. Once the Kabbalists had converted the Hebrew
text into anagrams, acrostics, and numerological riddles, they
discovered—or thought they discovered—all manner of hidden, esoteric knowledge. In particular, when Kabbalist 'decod-
ing' generated a series of apparently meaningless Hebraic
words, these were taken to be the names of angels. Hermes
Trismegistus and Moses, side by side: the planets and the
angels. It was a powerful pairing.

Pico della Mirandola certainly had some dangerously
unorthodox ideas, and he spent several years living under
the threat of papal condemnation, but he was perhaps more
a heretic than a magician. His 'magic' was of a philosophical, pious kind, more interested in achieving an ecstatic

vision than in finding buried treasure. But after his early and suspicious death, his ideas were taken up by others with more practical concerns. The most famous and notorious of these was the German scholar Cornelius Agrippa von Nettesheim, an unnerving magus whose despair over the fragility of all human learning was matched by a recurring hunch that hidden or occult knowledge might be the answer. His *De occulta philosophia* (1531–3) was not a conjurer's handbook (much to the frustration of those who believed its reputation and sought it out). Rather, it was a philosophical discussion of how Hermetic–Kabbalistic magic was possible. The earthbound magician, caught in the lumpish realm of the elements, might call on the higher spheres of the planets and stars, whose astral influences could be brought to bear on the sublunary world. And he could also call on the angels above the firmament, the pure spirits through whom the whole created order was governed. The angelic names of the Kabbalah became, as they had always threatened to, an incantation.

Agrippa's magic still had its spiritual side: he aimed in part at achieving a 'frenzy', by which he meant aligning his soul with an angel. Yet he had an eye to demons as well as angels. Indeed, he warned his readers that it was dangerous to deal exclusively with angels, whose fiery righteousness might swallow you up. A 'mixture of powers', he said coyly, would be more prudent. And those powers were being harnessed for bluntly practical purposes. Agrippa aspired to a whole range of magical techniques: using natural patterns in the four classical elements (earth, fire, water, and air) for divining the future, the manufacture of magical objects which drew on astral influences (talismans, perfumes, potions, and—of course—rings), and the summoning of angels or demons to provide knowledge for the magus, or work miracles on his behalf.

This kind of magic remained fearsomely esoteric and learned. Agrippa's astrological magic required some horribly complex mathematics, and of course his and all the other great texts of Renaissance magic were only available in Latin. Their ideas spread slowly, especially to backwaters such as England. It is usually assumed that Renaissance magic stayed in a Latin ghetto, that it remained largely theoretical, and that more run-of-the-mill magicians scarcely noticed the handful of learned newcomers. Certainly, it is only from the later sixteenth century that we start to find significant English scholars picking up the Renaissance tradition, men such as the Hermeticist Robert Fludd and the mathematician, astrologer, and conjurer of angels John Dee. But Renaissance magic's ideas and reputation could not be so easily contained. For one thing, Agrippa, at least, became notorious as a sorcerer. His name was as potent as that of his contemporary and fellow-countryman, the alchemist Johann Faustus. In the late 1540s even an Englishman, the hardline Protestant John Hooper, was concerned enough about Agrippa's book to want it banned. Moreover, both Kabbalistic and learned astrological ideas had already reached much wider audiences, as we shall see. But for one example of how Renaissance magic was escaping from its rarefied world, we can turn to Gregory Wisdom.

The second in the series of scams which Wisdom visited on Lord Henry was a supposed attempt to give him enchanted musical gifts. This, as Lord Henry remembered, was to have been done by conjuring 'the god Orpheus'. This ambition placed Wisdom squarely in Ficino's shadow. Along with the *Corpus Hermeticum*, Ficino had discovered a body of texts called the *Orphica*, which likewise dated from the second or third centuries AD but purported to be much older, and indeed to be the work of the mythical

Orpheus himself. Ficino saw Orpheus as the immediate spiritual heir of Hermes Trismegistus, and predecessor of Pythagoras (then more famed for his occult mysticism than for his geometry, although the two were closely linked). The *Orphica* contained incantatory hymns to the Sun and other heavenly bodies, which fitted cleanly into Ficino's emerging magical worldview, and indeed became central to it. Here, he believed, he had an exceptionally ancient religious-magical music, which could draw down the power of the planets by echoing the music of the spheres, those pristine harmonies which governed the intricate and perfect dance of the heavens. Ficino even went so far as to compose music with which to sing these hymns. The music of Jupiter, he suggested, was earnest and sweet; that of Venus (of course) voluptuous and wanton; that of Mars (equally clearly) harsh and threatening. These incantatory musics he played on an instrument which he confidently believed was an Orphic lyre. Pico della Mirandola enthusiastically took up Ficino's Orphic singing, blending it with the comparable Kabbalistic traditions of psalm-singing. Now there is no sign that Gregory Wisdom was engaged in anything so high flown, even if we allow that Lord Henry may have missed some of the subtleties of the ceremony. Yet at the very least, even if the connection is no more than the name Orpheus itself, that pretension to classicism shows that Wisdom knew something about what learned Renaissance magicians were supposed to do, and that he was trying, in a rough and ready way, to join in.

There is, in fact, only one major area of magical enterprise which Wisdom cannot be directly connected to: this is the slippery category of 'natural magic'. But it is still worth some attention, because it was one of the major conduits between the world of the learned magi and that of the tricksters.

'Natural magic' was the term Ficino used to describe all of his techniques, and even Agrippa claimed it for much of what he was attempting. This was the most 'scientific' face of early modern magic: it meant carrying out procedures which were in fact perfectly natural, but which merely appeared magical to the ignorant. In the 1970s, Arthur C. Clarke argued that 'any sufficiently advanced technology is indistinguishable from magic'. In the 1570s, the Italian astrologer Tommaso Campanella would not have put it quite that way, but he was an enthusiast for what he called 'real artificial magic', meaning mechanical devices, such as moving statues, which were in fact operated by hydraulic or pulley systems. Much of the work of herbalists was also seen as having a magical edge to it: in particular the preparation of poisons. When the friar in *Romeo and Juliet* prepared a potion which induced the appearance of death, an Elizabethan audience would have seen it as a work of natural magic.

However, Shakespeare's potions point us to one of the problems with much so-called natural magic. The practitioners of natural magic may have thought it natural, but modern science tells us that what it claimed to do was impossible. The pseudo-sciences of metoposcopy and physiognomy (which purported to discern someone's character and fortune from their appearance) were popular; Jonson's alchemists practised them, and Henry VIII argued against his bishops' attempts to condemn them. They were no more magical than the Victorian art of phrenology, which aimed to detect criminal tendencies by examining the precise shape of the skull; they were also no more reliable. And the Neoplatonist philosophies which Ficino and his successors spread suggested even more far-fetched possibilities. To Neoplatonists, the whole cosmos was an organic whole, in which invisible influences could connect apparently quite separate objects. The moon's power to move the seas in tides was the most spectacular example of such a spiritual influence, but the smaller scale miracle of magnetism was equally impressive and offered more practical hope to the would-be natural magician. Magnetism was cited in support of the common seventeenth-century medical technique called the weaponsalve. Theory suggested that when a weapon inflicted a wound, the connection between weapon and wound persisted after the weapon was withdrawn. Therefore, to treat the wound, the weapon had to be found and anointed with the same medicines as were used on the victim's body. Those with a more mundane view of the world looked askance at this. Yet its advocates argued passionately that it was not magic, but the leading edge of technology.

Indeed, in practice no one was entirely sure where magic began and ended. An unpleasant and anonymous fragment of sixteenth-century English magical advice describes a technique for finding stolen objects, in which angels were invoked to mould a soft wax figurine into the likeness of the thief. The author suspected, however, that the invocation of angels was not necessary, and that the process worked by 'ordinary sympathetical or magnetical' means. He tells us that he tested this hunch by making a similar wax figure of his own daughter, and discovered that—when the stars were correctly aligned— 'by putting a pin to the part of the image represented thereby, I could sensibly hurt her at my pleasure . . . or could procure her to sweat at my pleasure'. Having made this repulsive claim, he piously warned against invoking spirits unnecessarily when 'natural means' were available. He was willing to be a child abuser, but not, it seems, a conjurer.

Much the best-known form of natural magic, however, was alchemy. We have already met fraudulent alchemists, and they were notorious, but they did not succeed in discrediting the whole enterprise. Alchemy in early modern

Europe was somewhat like nuclear fusion today: a tantalizing mirage of a possibility, which promised untold benefits while presenting dizzying technical challenges. Chaucer's *Canon's Yeoman's Tale* told both sides of the story. As well as introducing the cynically fraudulent alchemist whom we met in Chapter 3, it described the miserable life of the true believer. This alchemist spends his days poring over the smelting fire, preparing ever more disgusting concoctions and buying esoteric equipment. His researches are a catalogue of disasters— his smelting-pot, for example, explodes under the heat, spraying his chamber with shards of hot metal. As he and his accomplices are drawn deeper into 'that sliding science', it makes its mark on them. 'Men may them know by smell of brimstone | For all the world they stink as a goat.' They bankrupt themselves, borrowing money against a promise eventually to be able to repay silver with gold. Worst of all, after every disappointment, the hope that the next experiment will bring success 'creepeth in our heart'. It was that relentless, merciless hope that 'will make us beggars at last'— a spirit of perpetual, bankrupting optimism which united alchemists with the gamblers whom some of them worked to defraud.

Chaucer, writing in the 1390s, could have been describing the career of the Somerset alchemist Thomas Charnock, who spent thirty years from the mid-1550s trying to manufacture the philosophers' stone, source of all alchemical elixirs. Accidents, burned apparatus, suspicious neighbours, poverty, nosy and incompetent suppliers, and outbreaks of war thwarted him. His mentor told him of a philosophers' stone hidden in a wall at Bath Abbey, but before he could find it, the wall was torn down, the rubble flung into a dungheap, and the dungheap spread over fields (where it proved a miraculously effective fertilizer). In 1574, despite all these setbacks,

Charnock believed that he had successfully made the lesser, 'white' variant of the philosophers' stone. But he could not repeat his success. He died in 1581, still believing enlightenment and riches were within his grasp. As Bishop Earle put it half a century later, a fascination with alchemy was 'a disease incurable, but by an abundant phlebotomy [bleeding] of the purse'.

Surprisingly, others claimed to have been more successful. An Oxford alchemist-conjurer named John Buckley was arrested in 1570 on suspicion of debasing coinage, a serious offence. His technique, as it emerged under interrogation, was to use a powder to extract metal from a silver coin without damaging its surface, and then to use a 'water' to add weight to the coin so that the change could not be detected. The operation required no more than the heat of a small fire and could be performed at home. Buckley persuaded a stationer named William Bedoe to buy the secret from him for a gold tablet worth £4. Bedoe did so, and remarkably enough, he was delighted with his purchase. When he too was arrested, he confessed that he had successfully used Buckley's technique to 'lighten' silver shillings and sixpences to the worth of £8 or more; overall he had extracted some two ounces of pure silver, which he had taken to a London silversmith. He was already proposing to sell the secret on. What was actually happening here is mysterious. The authorities were more interested in the criminal intent than the alchemical technique. The outcome of the case is unclear, but it did not look good for Buckley. His claim that he had only debased Spanish coins, not good English ones, was a threadbare defence.

His interrogators' credulity may seem surprising, but the best available theory, in the form of Neoplatonic philosophy and the Hermetic tradition in particular, said that transmuting

base metals into gold ought to be possible. The ideas of
Paracelsus, which so invigorated medicine in general and
surgery in particular during the sixteenth century, were profoundly alchemical in nature. Kings and princes, with their
deep pockets, were often ready to invest a little in alchemical
research, a gamble in the hope of spectacular returns. Alchemy
as such was illegal in England, but the crown was ready to
disregard the law in its own interest: more than twenty royal
licences to practice alchemy were granted during the fifteenth
century. Even Elizabeth I could have her interest piqued. In
1594, she was approached by an alchemist named Roloff Peter-
son, from the German city of Lübeck, who promised 'on the
peril of my head' to bring the sum of 40,000 thalers into the
English treasury, and who as an earnest of his good intentions
sent her certain crystals which (he claimed) represented eight
years' worth of work. Elizabeth was sufficiently intrigued to
make further inquiries.

Nothing came of this, but two years later another
German alchemist found a more willing patron: the duke
of Württemberg accepted one Georg Honauer's proposal to
transmute a ton of iron into gold. When, after much intricate
preparation, the exercise failed and Honauer tried to flee, he
was caught and hanged on an enormous, elaborate gallows
made from the ton of iron. However, the duke hanged him for
his attempt at escape, not for his failure. Apparently he still
believed that Honauer could have done the transmutation,
but had been trying to withhold the secret, whereas Honauer
was surprised by his failure and fled because he could not
understand where he had gone wrong. Tara Nummedal, a
historian who has studied fraud amongst alchemists, believes
that professional charlatans were very rare. Serious alchemists
were scathing about the tricksters who dabbled in their
profession, despising them as the 'goldbeetle's guild'. But

serious or not, success in this kind of 'natural magic' was as
elusive as in any other.

Alchemy was a magical sub-specialism, a cliquish world
tainted with the social stigma of manual labour and the literal
stench of foul admixtures. Far more respectable, pervasive,
alluring, and intellectually powerful was the subtle art of
astrology. And here we can rejoin Wisdom's own activities, for
astrology was a great leveller: it linked princes and peasants,
magi, cunning-men, and charlatans.

Astrology was an art with ancient roots—which, of course,
provided much of its appeal. It was grounded, not in the
mystical speculations of Neoplatonism, but in the blunt prac-
ticality of Aristotelian philosophy which had underpinned
the medieval revival of classical learning. When the new-
fangled communities of scholars called universities first took
shape in the eleventh century, astrology became part of their
core curriculum; the world's oldest university, at Bologna,
was a particular astrological stronghold. Like a good deal
of classical learning, astrology was not easily reconciled with
Christianity—an immutable fate written in the stars seemed
to contradict both human free will and God's sovereignty. But
medieval scholarship relished this kind of challenge and managed at least to contain, if not wholly to resolve the tension.
Astrology was simply too useful to discard. It overlapped with
both music and mathematics, but above all it was seen as necessary for the practice of medicine. If John and Gregory Wisdom wished to be taken seriously as physicians, they would
have had to learn a good deal of astrology. They would need
to know which were the propitious days to bleed patients, or
to administer purgative or emetic drugs; which signs of the
Zodiac governed which parts of the body; how to interpret
the chronology of a patient's illness; and how to protect their

patients against the particular ailments which each alignment of the stars threatened. John Hall, an Elizabethan physician who was jealous of ignorant empirics such as the Wisdoms, insisted that astrology was as important a part of medicine as was surgery or anatomy. And indeed, as astrology's fiercest English critic said in 1560, 'the most part of astrologers are by profession physicians'. So were all of its early publicists. Medicine and stargazing went together. It is no surprise that Lord Henry expected Wisdom to be skilled in astrology, nor to find that the Wisdoms were acquiring astrological texts.

Neoplatonists such as Ficino and (especially) Pico della Mirandola had little time for this sort of old-fashioned astrological frippery. Pico della Mirandola saw astrological attempts to foretell the future as near-blasphemous, and his writings became an ammunition store for those who disliked the art. But his distaste for traditional astrology was matched by an enthusiasm for his own brand of astral magic. Likewise, Ficino made talismans which bore the symbols of particular planets, to attract those planets' influences to patients with particular ailments. Agrippa's dizzying astrological mathematics had the same aim. So while Renaissance magic in its pure form might despise traditional astrology, all it succeeded in doing was giving the wider astrological enterprise both new credibility and a stronger tang of occultism. John Calvin—no friend of astrology—chose his words carefully when he lamented the revival in astrology's status: 'many which think themselves witty [wise] men, yea and have been so judged, are as it were bewitched therewith.'

In this new climate, mathematics became a more intoxicating science than it has ever been before or since. It was partly a code-word for more dangerous practices: when the French bishop Jean de Monluc decided in the 1550s that he wished to be instructed in 'the art of mathematics', it was clearly applied rather than pure maths which appealed to him. The tutors he found introduced him to a shepherd who owned two familiar spirits; de Monluc was sufficiently impressed that he presented this man to the King of France (who was horrified). But mathematics was not simply a smokescreen. Girolamo Cardano was one of the great mathematicians of his age: the author of the first Latin treatise on algebra, and a pioneer in the solution of cubic and quartic equations. He was also an accomplished physician, so famous that when the Archbishop of St Andrews was dangerously ill in 1551, he summoned Cardano all the way from Lyons to Scotland to attend him. (Cardano proved his worth by sensibly prescribing bedrest and a strict diet: this detox was enough to restore the exhausted Archbishop, whereas more gung-ho medical intervention could well have killed him.) And without any sense that this was incongruous, he was also a zealous astrologer, who was briefly imprisoned in 1570 for having attempted to cast Christ's horoscope. More embarrassingly, on his way home from Scotland in 1552, he visited the English court of the young King Edward VI. Asked to forecast the King's fate, Cardano predicted that he would live for another forty years. Edward in fact died a few months later, prompting Cardano to publish a soul-searching treatise in which he re-examined his original calculations and tried to work out where he had gone wrong. This was at least commendably honest.

Cardano's failure did not cost him the admiration of the English scholar John Cheke, whom he had met in London. Cheke and his friend Sir Thomas Smith were a pair of brilliant young classicists, steeped in Renaissance learning, who as young men had tried to revolutionize the teaching of Greek at Cambridge, and were now at the heart of Edward VI's government. Both were committed Protestants. And both were committed astrologers. Smith was always suspicious (and half-ashamed) of astrology, but at times flung himself into his calculations so obsessively that he went without sleep. Cheke also, apparently, prepared a detailed horoscope for his young king, although it does not survive. He also made a practice of consulting his own horoscope before travel—a habit which betrayed him in the end, when the stars did not warn him of the Catholic agents who captured him in 1556.

If these ornaments of learning could find nourishment in astrology, it is no surprise that lesser minds joined them. One notable enthusiast was King Henry VIII himself. He made the accomplished astrologer John Robyns his personal chaplain and enjoyed discussing the art with him (Robyns, diplomatically, complimented the King's insights). He argued with those of his bishops who wanted astrology condemned as superstitious. When his second wife, Anne Boleyn, was pregnant with the child who would eventually become Queen Elizabeth I, Henry—desperate for a son—consulted 'physicians, astrologers, sorcerers and sorceresses', who (of course) all provided the good news which their master wanted to hear. When Elizabeth became queen herself, the date of her coronation was chosen with reference to the astrologer–mathematician John Dee. And she, like her predecessors, testified to the importance of the subject by treating any unauthorized attempts to cast horoscopes for royalty as heinous, possibly capital crimes. We already, of course, know that the nobility and gentry were keen to exploit the services astrologers could give them. This is how Wisdom's client Sir Nicholas Wentworth came to be 'defrauded by his science of astronomy'. Nor was it only the well born. In the 1590s, the astrological physician Simon Forman made his name, and his fortune, providing astrological services for many hundreds of Londoners alongside his medical practice—although, unlike

Wisdom, he never persuaded the Royal College of Physicians to accept him.

The further we slither down the social scale, however, the more distant the rarefied and learned astrology of Cardano becomes. The pamphleteer William Fulke, who loathed astrology, mocked the fact that 'a great number of the busiest and most curious Astrologians in England understand no Latin at all'—the Wisdoms being among those. This kind of vernacular astrology was possible largely because of a stream of popular astrological texts which started gushing from England's printing presses in the 1530s and 1540s. The staple of printed astrology was the almanac, a cheap annual publication which provided a simple calendar overlaid with astrological predictions, varying in sophistication or ambition. The medical uses of astrology were to the fore here. Almanacs quickly became an essential public-health service. The very first English almanac to have an acknowledged author was published in 1545, by Andrew Boorde, who was, as he proclaimed on the title page, 'of physic doctor'; however, in view of the draconian 1542 Act against Conjurations, he avoided making any but the vaguest predictions. Boorde followed this with a quick guide to do-it-yourself astrological medicine, which gave instruction on matters such as when to bleed patients and when to bathe them. It warned (for example) that 'when the moon is in Aries, it is not good for no sick man nor sickly men to shave their head or beard, for every hair hath a hole by which the evil vapours be inhasted'. But it also ventured beyond the merely medical, explaining which days were propitious for sowing or harvesting, for building, or 'to speed matters with women' (Boorde was a former monk).

However, Boorde was soon overtaken in the astrological market by others. Another physician, John Securis, produced a profitable series of almanacs in the 1550s and 1560s; these went beyond merely medical matters to advise on good or inauspicious days for hunting, fishing, sending children to school, buying livestock, going to law, shearing sheep, hiring servants, or even trying on new clothes. His main rival in the almanac market was the Yorkshireman Anthony Askham, an astrologer with a sideline in medicine rather than vice versa. Askham's 1550 *Little treatise of astronomy, very necessary for Physic and Surgery* did the same as Boorde's earlier textbook, but rather more lavishly and authoritatively. His almanacs also contained marvellously precise predictions for the year ahead. So, for example, in 1555 he predicted a prevalence of 'catarrhs' in the winter, agues in the spring, dropsy for middle-aged women in the spring and summer. As to the weather, there was to have been rain and snow on 20 January 1555, sleet and rain on 27 and 28 February, 'some showers' on 26 March, and—a particularly bold prediction—hail on 29 and 30 July. As always with weather forecasts, repeated inaccuracy did not stop the punters coming back for more.

Because, of course, the real attraction of astrology was not its mystical claims, its intellectual pretensions, or even its medical usefulness, but its professed ability to foretell the future. That claim is always attractive, and never more so than in an age of unpredictable political upheaval such as the sixteenth century. The Tudor kings and queens may have used astrologers themselves, but they were thoroughly alarmed about their subjects' doing the same. Incautious stargazers and soothsayers were regularly liable to be given a taste of prison to teach them more circumspection. This is the likeliest explanation for Gregory Wisdom's imprisonment in 1553.

The prognosticator who caused the greatest stir of the century, however, was another physician–astrologer: the Frenchman Michel de Nostradamus. Nostradamus was lifted above the common herd of almanac-makers in part by the trademark verses in which he delivered his prophecies, lines of such marvellously tantalizing obscurity that the credulous have read their hopes or (usually) fears into them down to the present. In England, however, Nostradamus' career was made by his timing. He appeared as a public figure in late 1558 and 1559, at the same time as Elizabeth succeeded to the English throne and set about the dangerous business of trying to change England's religious complexion within and fend off French and other threats from without. Doomsaying prophecies—especially doomsaying prophecies uttered by a Catholic Frenchman—found ready ears in a nervous country. As regulation of the book trade wavered during the political transition, at least four different editions of works by Nostradamus were printed, all by different printers, vying for trade. One Protestant complained that 'this Nostradamus reigned here so like a tyrant with his soothsayings, that without the good luck of his prophecies it was thought that nothing could be brought to effect'. Another admitted that 'the whole realm was so troubled and so moved with the blind, enigmatical and devilish prophecies of that heaven-gazer Nostradamus' that even Protestants lost their courage. Even the new Archbishop of Canterbury was said (probably unjustly) to have been unnerved. It was partly in response to this panic that a new law against magical practice was enacted in 1563, to replace the long-repealed 1542 Act. But the boom in noble interest in astrology was lasting. In 1560 the preacher Laurence Humphrey lamented that astrology was 'ravenned, embraced, and devoured' by the nobility, men who would not stir themselves with any other branch of learning. And we have the testimony of one notably unlearned nobleman to prove him right. In 1562, one of the government's spies wrote a report on the countess of Lennox, a possible claimant to the English throne. Amongst her supporters, the report warned, was the earl of Westmorland: that is, none other than our old friend Henry, Lord Neville. A tutor in the Lennox household had written a commentary on Nostradamus' prophecies, interpreting them so as to flatter the countess. He then presented this to Westmorland, who was delighted with it, giving the tutor 'ten crowns, with great entertainment and thanks'. He was older, and perhaps a little wiser; but he was still a sucker for a soothsayer who would tell him what he wanted to hear.

For those who were inclined to moral panic, astrology was the magical equivalent of soft drugs: damaging in its own right, certainly, but more so because it could lure the unsuspecting and curious into much darker magics. The stony Protestant Anthony Gilby worried that students at the universities were beginning by dabbling in astrology, and then, finding that it 'will not serve their fond purposes', they 'must enter into Necromancy, and call some dead spirit forth of his grave with the blood of a swallow or a cat'. There was not only animal sacrifice, he warned, but secret ceremonies and super- stitions, rituals of purification, and the recital of incantations formed—blasphemously—from the names of God. This was the world of ceremonial and ritual magic, the invocation of spirits and conjuring of demons: arcane, blasphemous, and (it was universally believed) hideously dangerous. A tale from the 1580s tells of a group of friends who stumbled across a land surveyor's mathematical notes, full of diagrams. They were literate, but found it hard to decipher these strange symbols. As one tried to do so, another warned him, 'My friend, you were not best to read too far in that book, lest you fetch one up, that will ask what he shall do. And if you can appoint him nothing, neither know how to lay him down again, he will do much hurt.' The idea so alarmed them that they threw the book down and fled the building. Angels and demons were close at hand; one could reach out and touch them. This was a raw, perilous, and potentially terribly powerful magic. And as we shall see, Gregory Wisdom was deeply implicated in it.

Nor was it all preachers' and peasants' fears. Francis Coxe was a former monk who, early in Elizabeth's reign, tried to lend magical support to a group of Catholic plotters and was arrested trying to fly the country in 1561. He was pilloried in London, and, as part of his public repentance, wrote a book laying bare his former errors: the most complete first-hand account of ceremonial magic yet printed. The magician, he wrote, must make a spiritual pact of some kind. This was not the terrible Faustian bargain of selling his soul, but a promise (for example) to abstain from wine or from meat. When the demon appears, he must provide an offering or a sacrifice— perhaps a hallowed piece of wax, perhaps a bird, perhaps even a few drops of Christian blood. And for his own protection, he must also work from within a hallowed circle or pentangle, bolstered with all kinds of consecrated paraphernalia: drawn with special chalks, lit by a fire scented with special powders, while the magician himself bore a crown, sword, and sceptre, and uttered dreadful invocations. Yet all these protections were vain, Coxe warned: the demons would not be mocked, and would betray those who tried to summon them. A substantial part of his book was spent describing the sinister and disgusting deaths which various magicians had met at the Devil's hands.

Sensationalist scaremongering, this: but occasionally cases turned up in the courts which told similar stories. On 21 September 1590, two servants from Edmonton in Middlesex stumbled across two men in a field, who ran as if surprised in some wrongdoing. One of the two miscreants was caught, and was found to have 'certain Latin books' about his person.

Marching the suspect back to where he had been found, they discovered a makeshift shelter erected underneath a large tree. There were

> certain circles on the ground within the said cabin, and one of the said circles was laid about with parchment written upon with crosses. And by the said cabin we found a stool with divers pots by the same stool, and a red cock being dead by it; and against the said stool, a fair crystal stone with this word, 'Sathan', written on it.

Further tools of the conjurer's trade were inside. There were other writings, parchments, and a piece of gilded brass engraved with letters the servants could not read. There were various powders, and also some arsenic (when a bloodhound was brought it, it turned out that the suspect who had fled had scattered arsenic behind him as he ran, masking the scent). And there were the defensive devices of ritual magic: a cope and surplice to impart some protective holiness, and a sceptre and a 'fair broad sword ready drawn' to aid the conjurer in asserting his will over the spirits. The suspect whom they did catch was found to be wearing two small pictures under his clothes. On his back was a picture of Christ crucified; on his chest, a 'picture of serpents or such like'. This was not a case of youths fooling around: these would-be magicians were making, or working towards, a fairly well-planned attempt to summon the Devil himself.

Such a damningly circumstantial report is rare, but most of the ingredients found here can be paralleled in other accounts. The most famous, perhaps, is an Italian case, that of the great sculptor Bienvenuto Cellini, who in the 1530s fell in with a Sicilian necromancer-priest. According to Cellini's later account, this magician took advantage of Rome's atmospheric ruins, and conducted his conjuring one evening inside the

Colosseum. Cellini simply wanted a night with a particular girl, but this magician—who was evidently ambitious—summoned a whole legion of fiends, who filled the amphitheatre; indeed, he professed to be terrified by the number who had appeared, so much so that Cellini (who could not actually see any fiends) was badly spooked. Any scepticism was unjustified, however, since he got—and promptly discarded—the girl. Less effective was the do-it-yourself magic attempted by a Londoner named William Blomefield in 1546. He and his servant drew a conjurer's circle on the roof of his own house one night, hoping to summon 'one that shall come and carry us both away'. Everything should have been fine: he even had a 'book' to control the weather, and, he said ruefully, 'the worst is I shall needs destroy part of the house here'. But a London rooftop is not the world's most private place: they were spotted and arrested before the rituals could be completed.

Was this the kind of magic Wisdom was practising? We have more direct clues in another contemporary case. William Wycherley was a London tailor arrested on sorcery charges in 1549. The first allegations against him concerned an attempt to conjure spirits to find buried treasure—an activity which we have met before and will meet again. When questioned about this, he claimed that he had used an unconsecrated sword for the conjuring, and that as a result the procedure failed. He also admitted having provided a consecrated sword, sceptre, and ring to two others who also hoped to conjure for hidden treasure. But as further questions were asked, more damning evidence came to the surface. When interrogated on a second occasion, Wycherley admitted that ten years earlier, he and four others had assembled in a village in Sussex to conjure a spirit named *Baro*, an 'oriental or septrennial spirit'. Two of the others were clergymen, one described as the 'master operator'; a third member of the group he called 'the scryer of the crystal stone'. They had drawn a circle, which he called the *Circulus Salamonis*, and had used holy water, a consecrated sword, and a consecrated ring to control the spirit. The spell failed, insofar as Baro did not appear, but there was 'a terrible wind and tempest'. A year later, at Yarmouth, he had also participated in a group trying to conjure a spirit, in this case one named (improbably) 'Ambrose Waterduke': they used 'the great circle, with the sword and ring consecrated'. Again, however, the effort failed, this time because one of their number—'an old priest'—was so terrified that he bolted during the procedure. Wycherley swore he had never attempted full-scale conjuring of spirits again.

These are fragmentary, unreliable, and unsatisfactory accounts, but they tell us enough. The similarities to Gregory Wisdom's magic are plain: his attempts to enchant a ring by conjuring spirits, and to find buried treasure with spiritual assistance. Just how deeply Wisdom was involved in magic of this kind, however, becomes clearer if we look at the theory behind it. Wycherley's reference to the 'circle of Solomon' makes it unmistakable that his magic was informed by the single most influential text of medieval magic: the *Clavicula Salomonis*, the 'Key of Solomon', a Jewish text of Kabbalistic magic much copied, altered, amended, and imitated by Christian magicians. This claimed to be the secret magical testament of King Solomon himself—the king whose proverbial wisdom was sharpened with a salty tang of unholiness, for he spent his last years whoring after false gods. It made him irresistible to magicians.

Dozens of variant manuscripts of the *Clavicula* survive, some of them still outwardly Jewish, some Christianized. There are common elements: ritualistic invocations of the many names of God and of the angels, the prescription of enormously elaborate preparations and equipment, the use of circles and other protective magic when spirits are being summoned, and—not least—the thoroughly mundane and selfish purposes for which spirits are summoned. Sometimes animal sacrifice is mentioned, but human sacrifice is rarely even implied; at most, a magician may be expected to use his own or another's blood to write spell-texts. The need for ritualized writing and rewriting of the text is one of the reasons why the Solomonic texts are so varied, and why no one attempted to print them until modern times: the text itself was a magical object, and could only be fully effective if prepared according to the correct ritual. The ceremonial complexity of Solomonic magic was, one modern historian has concluded, 'like the worst sort of obstacle-race'. It was not just expensive and labour-intensive; it was almost impossible to be certain of getting it right. This was no doubt frustrating, but it also supplied a ready explanation for failure.

The accounts of Wisdom's dealings with Lord Henry strongly suggest he was influenced by the Solomonic tradition. To make a magic ring by conjuring angels; to summon a spirit to grant musical talents; to send a spirit to find hidden treasure—all of these are well-established parts of the Solomonic repertoire. But there is also more direct evidence. In Chapter 2 we saw that when John Wisdom died in 1562, he left his son Gregory a book called 'the practice of Damell', which I have tentatively identified with a text in the British Library called 'the Dannel'. The *Dannel* is a detailed and revealing text of magic, set firmly within the Solomonic tradition, and it provides a unique window into the Wisdoms' magical world.

The title makes the Solomonic and Kabbalistic connection clear: 'Dannel' was the name given in the apocalyptic book of Enoch to an archangel. He was one of the leaders of the two hundred rebel angels who lusted after the daughters of men in the days before the Flood, who fathered giants, and who taught occult knowledge to humanity. Under this potent name, the book begins by proclaiming that it teaches 'the doctrine of all experiments in general'—*experiments* being the *Clavicle*'s common word for spells and rituals. In particular, it promises to teach how to use spirits to spread either love or hatred amongst chosen individuals; how to summon demons; how to use spirits to consecrate a range of objects, such as coins, wax images, or rings; and how to find hidden treasure. In classically Solomonic style, it lays out rules for the magician's careful preparations. As well as a rigorous regime of abstinence and personal hygiene before beginning his 'experiment', the magician must ensure that the stars are in the right alignment (the astrological conditions laid out are complex), and also that there is good weather: cloudy skies imperil the whole operation. This was because demons apparently enjoy basking in sunlight. We read that they will appear the more gladly if the 'experiment' is carried out in a secluded court-yard, a 'fair sweet garden', or a room brightly lit with a south-facing window; or, alternatively, in bright moonlight, because the success of the conjuration depended in any case on the phases of the moon.

When we come to the actual rituals of conjuration, we find, again, that a conjurer's circle is at the heart of it. Solomonic texts typically included drawings of pentagrams, and the *Dannel* has some particularly ornate ones (see Figs. 12 and 13). As well as being drawn on the ground, these symbols were to be carved onto the magician's staff, along with the names of God. The magician was to step into the pentagram, to kneel facing east, and to say a brief prayer explaining to God why he was summoning a spirit. It was done 'not to opprove thy power ... [but] to get therewith my board and necessaries'.

12. A conjurer's circle illustrated in the *Dannel*.

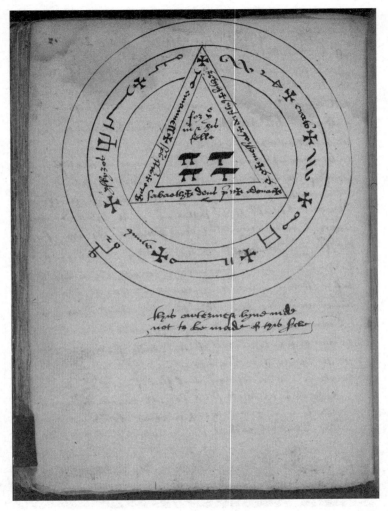

13. Another conjurer's circle from the *Dannel*.

The magician did not think of himself as a blasphemous meddler, but as an ordinary fellow simply trying to make ends meet. After this brief prelude, he was to turn to face south, and utter a much longer invocation. This consists of a series of commands issued to a demon, issued peremptorily and in the many names of God. Indeed, at the end of an exhaustive list of the divine names culled from Scripture, the rite adds a catch-all clause, commanding the demon 'by all other names that ever were able of man to be spoken or thought'. The demon is also informed, at some length, about the eternal and inescapable nature of its punishment in Hell. Once this lengthy text had been read, the demon was supposed to appear, but the book adds: 'And if he be not come, read it over again.' Even a third reading might sometimes be necessary. If this seems anticlimactic, however, the book was keen to warn its users that they were engaged on an extremely dangerous enterprise. If summoning a spirit to find hidden treasure, we read, one must stand in the circle facing north, pointing a naked, consecrated sword to the south, holding a consecrated sceptre in the right hand and wearing a consecrated ring on the little finger of the left hand. Then the words of conjuration should be said: 'but beware of looking in thy book, for then thou shalt be in great danger.' If one did not maintain eye contact with the spirits at all times, they might break loose.

The *Dannel*'s Solomonic nature is unmistakable—it is filled with references to Solomon's temple, book, wisdom and, of course, his key—but it varies from the norm in some significant ways. Not least, it is in English: this is a dumbed-down magic book, for those who wanted the power of ancient ritual but could not cope with Latin. Moreover, it is thoroughly Christianized: the names of God include numerous references to Christ and to the Trinity. The self-justifying cant of the initial prayer is also not part of the mainstream Solomonic tradition, although as we shall see, this kind of veneer of religiosity can be significant. And the *Dannel* also contains one peculiarity, a very unusual detail in contemporary books of magic. When discussing the best time of day for conjuring angels to perform love spells, it insists that this be done during the small hours of the night, for if dawn breaks before the ceremony is concluded the ritual will fail. However, it warns, night-time conjurers of angels should also avoid 'the hour matitinial'—the hour when matins, the pre-dawn monastic office, was said. 'For then spirits ... come to holy church, ... and so the time of matins, it profiteth not at all for the caller.' This was almost exactly how Wisdom explained to Lord Henry his difficulties in making a magical ring.

None of this proves categorically that the 'Practice of Damell' which the Wisdoms owned actually was the *Dannel*. What it does prove beyond reasonable doubt is that Gregory Wisdom was more than a physician and a con-man. His activities show that he genuinely knew something about magic—about Renaissance magic, but much more about ceremonial magic in the Solomonic tradition. If he had not read the *Dannel*, he had obviously read something pretty like it. And what that suggests—though it cannot prove—is that, like many tricksters, he was also a believer.

We can, then, trace the intellectual ingredients of Wisdom's magic: a dash of Renaissance spice and a leavening of astrology, mixed into a solid lump of ritual conjuring. But in some ways this misses the point. The Renaissance magi, some of the more mystical alchemists, and even the more respectable astrologers, may have seen their magics as spiritual or intellectual enterprises. But for most people, magic was bluntly practical, a means to an end—usually an end which involved hard cash. And there is no doubt which side of that divide Wisdom stood on (let alone Henry, Lord Neville). If we want to understand his magic, its intellectual origins are no more important than its context. The services he was offering to Lord Henry were widely available.

Take, for example, his first scheme: to make a magic ring for dicing. We have already seen how rings were a recurring feature of ritual magic. It is hardly surprising. Medieval society was accustomed to rings being marks of authority, of identity, or of office (signet rings, for example); and the sacral significance of the ring, symbolically never-ending, was well established from its use in the sacrament of marriage. Legends of magical rings were common currency. It was said, for example, that one of the emperor Charlemagne's concubines had bewitched him with a magic ring, causing him to follow her 'as a dog after a bitch'. When she died, a nobleman took the ring, only to find that the emperor's attentions were now transferred to him. Finding this 'tedious' (as we might imagine), the nobleman eventually threw the ring into a well in Aachen, whereupon Charlemagne settled in the city and never left it again.

I have only found one other case of a ring being used for gambling: a fragment of a document from the early 1580s refers to a Dr Elkes, a Suffolk conjurer who had conspired with another man 'for a Spirit to be enclosed in a Ring for play'. The ring was engraved with Hebrew letters, the magicians' trademark. However, the question of how to tip the gaming tables was one which exercised other magicians too. A man named Alen, arrested in 1549, had amongst his papers some instructions for astrological gambling (this was what Lord Henry had initially expected Wisdom to offer him). It did not sound very promising, however: he merely suggested that 'when thou wilt go forth to play at the Cards

and Dice', you should ensure that you begin the game at precisely the right time, and you should face towards the moon,
preferably with moonlight actually touching you. Stronger
medicine was available for those who wanted it. A favoured
technique, apparently, was to conjure a familiar spirit into an
insect, which could then be brought into the gamblers' den to
provide secret advice. The preacher Anthony Gilby believed it
was commonplace 'to have a Bee in a box to teach them to play
at the Dice and Cards'. In the 1570s, a small business supplying
'dicing flies' was allegedly being run by no less a figure than the
Master of Balliol College, Oxford, Adam Squier. A group of
men from Somerset complained that he had sold them a fly 'to
go to dice withal', but instead of winning as he had promised,
they were in fact beggared. With pleasing innocence, they
laid an indignant complaint before their local magistrates, in
Nether Stowey. There is no record as to whether they were
refunded for the fly, but the complaint caused a considerable
stink in Oxford, and for a while looked as if it might cost
Squier his job.

Another of Wisdom's schemes which was widely paralleled
was his attempt to find buried treasure. This was perhaps the
early modern period's ultimate get-rich-quick scheme, less
technical and arcane than alchemy and offering rewards as
great as avarice could dream of. Yet it had its drawbacks.
Digging in the open, invariably at night, nerves jangling with
fear of spirits, meant that treasure-hunting was not for the
faint of heart. In about 1547 William Wycherley, whom we
have already met as a Solomonic conjurer, became involved
in an attempt to discover treasure in (of all places) Fulham,
on the outskirts of London. But during the night, while he
and his accomplices were digging, 'there came by them along
the highway a black, blind horse'—how they could tell it
was blind is not explained, but in any case they scattered,

terrified. Similarly, in 1527, a man named John Curson was convinced by a 'cunning man' that he would find £3000 in gold buried in two pots under a wayside cross near Kettering, in Northamptonshire. He was warned, however, that two spirits guarded the money. He and two workmen tried to dig at the chosen spot one night, but as soon as their tools broke the surface 'they heard such a lumbering within the ground' that the workmen fled.

In the event, Curson himself returned for another attempt, this time bringing no less than six labourers. The spirits, thus outnumbered, kept their counsel, but they did not give up their treasure. Curson's determination partly reflected the investment he had already made in the scheme. He had paid his 'cunning man' more than £6 to be told about this supposed treasure. Others paid in a different currency. The full-scale Faustian pact—selling one's soul to the Devil—existed more in the fears of the righteous than in the practice of the wicked, but where demonic pacts of some kind were attempted, discovering hidden treasure was almost invariably their purpose. What united all these schemes, of course, was their failure. Anthony Gilby mocked the discomfiture of magicians who 'can find no money under crosses'.

We are closer to Wisdom's own practice with the case of John Buckley and William Bedoe, the alchemists arrested in 1570 for debasing coinage (see p. 119). The two men had first met because Buckley had a reputation for skill in matters uncanny, and Bedoe had sought him out. Bedoe believed that some stolen money, perhaps £8 or £10, was hidden somewhere in a house in Brenchley, in Kent. Buckley was persuaded to visit the site and divine for the money. When this failed, Buckley, 'having a certain crystal stone about him,' attempted to call a spirit named *Oriens* 'to see whether he would appear in the said crystal to give him to understand whether there were any money hid in the said house or not'. This says something about Buckley's magical background—*Oriens* was the name of the demon of the east in the Solomonic tradition—but it is the use of a crystal which is more striking. Wisdom, too, had claimed that he had a spirit which he kept in a crystal, and which he used to reconnoitre buried treasure.

Crystals were not widely used in magic across Europe, but they were commonplace in England. We have already met the Edmonton conjurers whose crystal was engraved with the name 'Sathan'. The fainthearted conjurer William Wycherley admitted that he was more comfortable using a crystal than practising full-scale demon-summonings. He had used a crystal more than a hundred times to invoke a spirit called *Scariot*, who had helped him find stolen property. It usually worked, he claimed, but he admitted that he was not as good as some other conjurers at preventing the spirit from lying to him. He then proceeded to name some of these other conjurers and 'scryers of the glass', such as an embroiderer named Lowth who 'useth the crystal stone, and goeth about daily to dig for treasure'. Crystal-gazing was, in fact, a central part of any English magician's repertoire. Ben Jonson mocked it; so did the most redoubtable contemporary critic of magic, Reginald Scot. In 1467, a Yorkshire magician accused of sorcery with a crystal was hauled before the Archbishop of York: at that date George Neville, a cousin of the earls of Westmorland.

We have now reached the most workaday, pragmatic, and unlearned magic of the lot: the humdrum activities of local cunning-men and diviners, providing simple services to ordinary clients. Theories of magic, of whatever kind, seem quite out of place in this cheerful cocktail of supernatural practice. What mattered was what worked, or was thought to work.

From this point of view, the main function of magic in early modern England was as a lost-property service, and in particular as a means of recovering stolen goods. This was how William Wycherley made his living: not only with his nearly tame spirit, but also by using more humdrum methods of divination. He described, as an example, being approached by a woman who had had ten shillings stolen. He asked her to write the names of the people she suspected on small slips of paper. These slips were then rolled up and one was placed in a hollow space inside a large key. He then took up a Latin psalter, and opened it to Psalm 49 (Psalm 50 in most English Bibles), verse 18 of which begins *Si videbis furem*—'if you see a thief'. Laying the key across that verse of the psalm, he held the book while the woman spoke aloud an altered version of the verse. Then a different slip of paper, with a different name, was place inside the key and the procedure was repeated. 'And when this verse was said over one of the names...the book and key turned round.' That was the thief. Asked how often he had carried out this little ritual, Wycherley replied 'that he cannot express how many the times; for people are so importunate upon him daily for this purpose, that he is not able to avoid them, but keepeth himself within his door.'

And indeed, we have plenty of other evidence that such everyday magical services were much sought after. The trick with the book and key was very widespread, as was a similar technique in which a sieve was balanced on the point of a pair of shears—when the thief's name is spoken, the sieve turns suddenly. That technique goes back to, at least, the third century BC. Like that more modern invention, the Ouija board, these were excellent ways of amplifying the unspoken or even unconscious suspicions of the participants, and giving them a little supernatural legitimacy. Other techniques were even more open to nudges. Alen, the small-scale prophet arrested in 1549, had his own technique for detecting thieves: to write a simple and near-nonsensical charm assembled from Christian terms on a piece of parchment, and to go to sleep with this on or under your head. While you slept, he promised, 'thou shalt have a vision and knowledge who hath thy thing'. As an alternative, he offered a lie-detecting formula, based on the number of letters in the suspected liar's name and on the days of the week; it produces the invariable result that those who lie on Tuesdays, Fridays, and Saturdays are truthful for the rest of the week, and vice versa.

This sort of thing may seem risible, and indeed it was much mocked, but it was also much used. It provided the invaluable service of providing apparent confirmation of people's pre-existing suspicions. And in a world with virtually no policing and even less forensic science, the recovery of stolen goods was a serious problem. Preachers agreed that magical divina-tion and thief-taking was 'much used' and 'are marvellously increased', and that 'a great many of us do…when we be in trouble, or sickness, or lose any thing…run hither and thither to wizards, or sorcerers, whom we call wise men'. Princes as well as peasants exploited this kind of magic. Wycherley had been hired to find a lost item—apparently a silver plate—for none other than Edward Seymour, Duke of Somerset and Lord Protector of England. He summoned his spirit to his crystal in the presence of a series of courtiers, some of them impeccably 'godly' reformers; and gave them information which led to the successful recovery of the plate.

Such successes kept the business coming, but they also prompted murmurs of foul play. Alen may have been an indif-ferent magician, but he was closely linked to a notoriously crooked gambler, Tom Morgan, who testified that Alen had taught him techniques for winning at dice. Indeed, Morgan's testimony suggests that Alen's magical activities were a smokescreen for murkier enterprises. Alen apparently rented rooms in several different places across London, where clients came to consult with him and 'where the ruffling roisters the dicers made their matches'. It was said that women came to him under the pretence of seeking lost or stolen goods, but in truth so that he could arrange assignations for them; he had 'a chamber...where was many things practised'. The officer who arrested him claimed that he received death threats from the 'lords and ladies, gentlemen, merchants, knaves, whores, bawds, and thieves' who had been Alen's clients. We are back in the underworld.

These were scandalous, but ultimately venial offences. Wisdom had, of course, been involved in a much graver crime: attempted murder. Cases of this kind were rare, but attracted considerable attention when they took place. In January 1538, a London servant named Fulke Vaughan spotted a disturbing object in the churchyard next to his master's house. It looked to him like a baby's body, wrapped in a shroud and half-buried. He and the church clerk unwrapped the winding sheet, nervously, only to discover something almost worse: a wax image of a child, with two pins stuck through it. Vaughan, interestingly, immediately knew whom to go to for advice: a scrivener in Crooked Lane, who clearly had a reputation as a magician. This man confirmed that the image was indeed an attempt at magical murder, but he was scornful about it. 'He that made it was not his craft's master, for he should have put it either in horse dung or in a dunghill.' Then the intended victim would indeed have been killed. There is no evidence either that anyone of any significance was involved, or that anyone at all was actually hurt, but the matter was taken extremely seriously, and some very senior officers of state became involved in the investigation—although without any success.

Similar cases crop up occasionally through the century. In 1543, a Kentish woman who bore a grudge against her neighbour Elizabeth Celsay set about some particularly noisome malevolent magic. She planned to make 'a fire upon the dung of the said Elizabeth' (we are not told how she would get hold of this) and to drip the wax of a holy candle into the fire: this, she said, would make Elizabeth's bottom 'divide into two parts'. Quite what that means is not clear, but it does not sound pleasant. More ambitiously, in 1589, a Mrs Dewse was arrested for trying to murder an entire bench of magistrates. They had, she said, robbed her and tried to drive her husband from his offices. With the help and advice of a conjurer, she too had made wax images of them and driven pins through them, apparently hoping to torment them before she finally killed them.

What is striking about Mrs Dewse's crime is the status of her intended victims. She was using magic to strike at the powerful and well-protected, men she wished ill of but would be unable to reach in any other way. It is a common feature of attempted magical murders. Most notoriously, in 1538 a Yorkshirewoman named Mabel Brigge tried to kill the best protected man in England, King Henry VIII. The brutal repression in the North of England which followed the rebellion of 1536–7 meant feelings were running high, and a small group of conspirators had hatched a plan. Brigge was to fast for three days while praying for the deaths of the King and of the duke of Norfolk. She had done this once before, she claimed, and the intended victim had broken his neck before the fast was concluded. She called the ritual a 'black fast', and also a 'fast of St. Trinian'—the Irish saint who in the twentieth century became (fittingly enough) synonymous with cheerfully homicidal schoolgirls. There was little cheer for Brigge and her associates, however. Neither King nor duke died. One of the conspirators then told his parish priest of the plot in confession. The priest, valuing his skin above the sanctity of the sacrament, reported them all. The leading conspirators were swiftly found guilty of treason; Brigge alone of them was executed, by hanging, drawing, and quartering, at York on 7 April 1538.

Brigge's motive was political, but most attempted magical murders amongst the ruling classes were more pragmatic affairs, centred on hopes of inheritance. This was true of a previous attempt at royal murder: the duchess of Gloucester's attempt either to predict or to bring about Henry VI's death in 1441 was driven by her hopes that her husband would then become king. On a smaller scale, in 1560 two sorcerers were arrested for trying to murder William St Loe, a member of Queen Elizabeth's household. They had been procured, it turned out, by his brother and daughters, who feared that his new marriage (to the formidable dynast Bess of Hardwick) might produce a son and so disinherit them all. This was not too different from the spirit in which Henry, Lord Neville apparently consented to the murder of his wife and father.

Nor was Lord Henry the first Neville to tangle himself in this kind of conspiracy. A junior branch of the family held the title of Lord Latimer. John Neville, the third Lord Latimer, who died in 1543, had at least twelve and perhaps as many as fifteen younger siblings. Impressive as this kind of fecundity was, it had its problems, for some of those siblings were inclined to chafe. In 1531–2 one of them, William Neville, became involved in a murky plot aimed at securing the title for himself. It is not clear whether William actually plotted his brother's murder, or merely listened avidly to prophecies of his untimely death. What is certain is that he attached himself to a sorcerer called Richard Jones, who fed him a series of dreams and predictions: that there would be a battle in which his brother would be killed, that if he were on the spot when his brother died he would become Lord Latimer, and that he would thereafter succeed to the glorious and long-extinct earldom of Warwick, last held by another Neville, Warwick 'the Kingmaker'. This was a particularly dangerous hope, since noble titles were in the King's gift, yet Jones spoke of Henry VIII dying or being overthrown when William came to the earldom. Jones also (to complete the parallel with Wisdom) foretold that William's wife would die and that he would make a splendidly lucrative new match with a teenage bride.

Like Lord Henry's case, this one briefly threatened to be very nasty. Under the draconian new laws, the prophecies which the conspirators had bandied about were almost certainly treason. But Henry VIII's government was sometimes able to tell the difference between dangerous plots and dreamers' tittle-tattle, so—as would happen fifteen years later—the plotters endured nothing worse than a taste of prison. Indeed Jones, a resourceful man, even offered his services to the Crown as an alchemist. And in the end, the significance of this episode is less the political upheaval that it briefly threatened and more its testimony to what a restless member of the Neville family might be willing to believe. Like Wisdom, Jones offered a full range of magical services to his eager client. They had spoken of Cornelius Agrippa's magic, and also of the medieval astrologer–philosopher Roger Bacon, a man with a largely unjustified reputation as a magician. Jones also claimed to be able to use the magic of Solomon to make rings which would win the favour of princes. William Neville even set out at one stage to make himself a cloak of invisibility, out of linen and leather treated with an unpalatable powder made largely from the bones of horses. It is hardly surprising that he was not seen as genuinely dangerous.

Magic in the sixteenth century was a world of contradictions: theoretical as against practical magic, learned against popular, honest against fraudulent. Those contradictions mean that it was and remains a slippery subject, hard to pin down. It was perhaps impossible even for the most credulous to believe everything that was claimed for it, not least because of its own inconsistencies. It was also very difficult to dismiss it as pure nonsense, so powerful were the philosophical arguments for some kinds of magic. For those who wished to make a living from magic, it was precisely these contradictions that were their meat and drink. It allowed magicians to believe (not wholeheartedly, perhaps, but to believe) in the scams they were selling; and nothing convinces a client like sincerity. Men like Richard Jones, William Wycherley, or— maybe more effortlessly than any of them—Gregory Wisdom could move between theory and practice, high learning and low cunning, and truth and lies. Their clients did not know where the boundaries were, and neither, it seems, did they.

5

The Preacher

THE last thread of this story leads us out of the secret worlds of Tudor England into the glare of publicity and of historical attention. The sixteenth century was defined, in its own eyes as well as in ours, by the traumatic religious convulsion which we call the Reformation. It is a neat word for a set of events which were by turns exhilarating, appalling, frightening, and (above all) confusing for those who lived through them. It is usually remembered as the point at which England abandoned its traditional Catholicism in favour of the novelty called Protestantism—a transition which is often seen as a movement from superstition to rationality, or from authoritarianism to liberalism. It did not seem quite like that to those who lived through it. Gregory Wisdom's exploits might at first sight seem to have little to do with religion, but the Reformation provided more than the context in which he lived. He will introduce us to a side of the Reformation which is not so familiar, and help us to see the religious upheavals of the sixteenth century in a new light.

To tell this side of the story, we have to introduce a member of the Wisdom family whom we have not yet met. Robert Wisdom was John Wisdom's nephew and Gregory's cousin. He was, it seems, the white sheep of the family. He too found himself in trouble with the law in the 1540s—indeed, in much more real danger than his relations—but for very different reasons. Robert had pursued a career, not in medicine, but in the Church. He quickly proved himself (as we might expect from a Wisdom) to be able, ambitious, and combative. Like his relatives, he lacked the benefit of a university education, but in the late 1530s he nevertheless landed himself a series of plum church postings, first in Oxford, then in Essex. He was also being invited to preach regularly in London. But his rapid rise was attracting unwelcome attention, because Robert Wisdom was an outspoken advocate of the new, controversial doctrines of Protestantism.

These were perilous times. Henry VIII had fallen out bitterly with the Pope, in an argument which began but did not end with royal marriage plans. Eventually, in 1534, Henry had unilaterally declared the English Church independent. In place of the Pope—now officially described as the 'bishop of Rome', and vilified—the English Church was to be headed by the King himself. This *coup d'état* began an exceptionally baffling period in England's religious history. Henry was not by any means a Protestant. He was repelled by the radical doctrines of Martin Luther; he was appalled by the even more radical ideas of Huldrych Zwingli, John Calvin, and their Swiss followers. Protestants were liable to be charged with heresy in England for as long as Henry lived, and public burnings continued until the very end of his reign. Yet his break with Rome was only possible because Protestant territories in Germany and elsewhere had paved the way. Indeed, Henry and the German Lutherans made repeated attempts at a military alliance. And Henry's new 'Church of England' was not quite Catholic any more, despite what most of its members might have wanted. You could not cut off the old Church's head without expecting some consequences. And while Henry himself was no Protestant, some of his clergy and advisers were. They pressed their agenda piecemeal, exploiting the King's capricious goodwill and short attention span as far as they dared. They won some important victories, but it was a dangerous game, and the rules were always changing.

This was, then, a period of bewildering religious flux, when the certainties which had framed the lives of good Christians (and of bad Christians) for close on a thousand years were being torn up. Nothing very clear was yet being put in their place. Instead, dozens of different, overlapping shades of possibility were appearing. The direction of change was unclear and official orthodoxies were subject to alarming lurches. Most English people found ways of surviving this process, usually with more discretion than valour. Some—including the Wisdoms—found ways of prospering. The Wisdoms' adventures give us a snapshot of what it meant to live and work during such a chaotic, confusing, creative era, and tell us something about how that chaos eventually resolved itself into a new order.

Robert Wisdom, the clergyman, faced these challenges with a forthright, brittle self-confidence. His partisan Protestantism quickly won him a reputation for being provocative. He had a brief run-in with the Bishop of Lincoln in 1537. In 1541 the Bishop of London moved against him more seriously. The Bishop's men were sent to take notes at his sermons, and when they had enough evidence to charge him with heresy, he was arrested. Robert was persuaded to forswear his supposed errors, but when released he continued preaching much as he had before. In 1543 he was arrested again, as part of a larger crackdown against Protestants. This time he expected to face the usual punishment for relapsed heretics: death by burning. Instead, he was allowed once again to recant, but this second recantation was public, abject, and humiliating.

After this disaster, Robert Wisdom took his leave of London. He went first of all to stay with a friend in Staffordshire, but remained on the move for the next three years or more, never spending more than a few months in one place. Now banned from preaching, he poured his energies into writing, tortured with guilt for his inconstancy. During the next major crackdown against Protestants in 1546, he fled abroad to Germany before he could be arrested. But for Robert, as for so many others, the death of Henry VIII in January 1547 meant new hope. The new minority government ruling in the name of Edward VI began to ram through a full-scale Protestant Reformation. Robert returned to England to take part in the revolution, and briefly he seemed destined for great things. He was spoken of as a possible Archbishop of Armagh—perhaps reflecting the new regime's desperation to find any English Protestants who would accept Irish bish-oprics. But in the event, Edward VI died before Robert could climb very far up the greasy pole. The accession of Queen Mary, a loyal Catholic, drove him back into German exile. When Elizabeth I became Queen in 1558, and the world changed yet again, Robert returned to resume his career, but his glorious future was now behind him. His health was shaky, and he died in 1568. Still, he lived out his last few years as a pillar of the reformed Church of England. He became Archdeacon of Ely, was invited to preach before the Queen, and sat in Convocation, the Church's parliament. He even contributed a few, much-mocked verses to the *Whole Book of Psalms*, the English hymn book of which something like a million copies were printed in the century after 1560.

Robert Wisdom might seem poles apart from his kinsmen Gregory and John. They represented everything that good Protestants like Robert loathed. Quite aside from the fraud, gambling, and prostitution, of which no Christian priest could approve (at least not in public), the Protestant establishment had, as we shall see, a particularly dim view of magic. Robert himself rarely addressed the subject, but we know he preached against the belief in ghosts—'souls departed do not come again, and walk, and play bo-peep with us'. Gregory, by contrast, would probably have put a sheet over his head and played bo-peep himself if he had thought one of his clients would believe it. And yet, the connections between the magicians and the preacher run deeper than we might think.

When Robert was first arrested, in July 1541, he initially refused to back down. The Bishop of London, Edmund Bonner—an ill-tempered but not fanatical bishop, who had a degree of sympathy for his prisoner—permitted Robert to receive two visitors: a Protestant publisher named Edward Whitchurch, and his uncle, John Wisdom. The bishop made plain to the visitors just how dangerous Robert's situation was. He could potentially be burned as an obstinate heretic. Whitchurch and John Wisdom therefore set themselves to persuade Robert to back down (with John, it seems, taking the lead). They warned him that because he was 'of a weak complexion', imprisonment would be the death of him: in that sentiment we can hear the confident voice of the self-educated physician. And they added that if he died, or was forced into a public retraction, he would be both silenced and discredited. Robert crumbled under the pressure, which he later regretted, but his uncle and his friend were right: they may well have saved his life.

That an uncle should support his imprisoned nephew is perhaps unsurprising, regardless of ideology. Blood is thicker than water. But it is hard to avoid the conclusion that John favoured Robert's preaching as well as his person. In 1541, he appeared in the company of Whitchurch, a known Protestant ideologue. In 1543, when Robert was again arrested, and this time forced into a public recantation, his uncle stood by him more publicly. John and two others stood as sureties for Robert, guaranteeing to cover the costs of his imprisonment to the tune of £40 if necessary. The two other sureties were both Protestant radicals.

The only direct testimony we have as to John Wisdom's own beliefs points in the same direction. His will was drawn up on 17 July 1559, when the new, Protestant regime of Elizabeth I was still unsteady on its feet. But when John included (as was normal) a religious preamble to his will, it was unambiguous. He bequeathed his soul to God alone—no mention of the Virgin Mary or the saints, itself a break from tradition—and emphasized that he trusted 'through the merits of Jesus Christ's most bitter and precious passion to have full and clear remission of my sins'. This was a succinct summary of the central Protestant belief that salvation comes *only* through faith in Christ, and nothing else. One of the witnesses to John's will was 'W. Cunningham'—probably William Cunningham, a much-published physician–astrologer who was also an outspoken Protestant.

The family's association with Protestantism does not end there. The Wisdoms were not Londoners of long standing, but apparently came from the town of Burford in Oxfordshire. Burford was one of the Thames Valley towns which had long been a cradle of the medieval English heresy known as Lollardy. Lollards were not Protestants, but they did anticipate some Protestant ideas—in, for example, their violent dislike of Catholic ritual and their insistence on using the Bible in English rather than Latin. Many Lollards embraced Protestantism very readily when it appeared in England. Some at least of the Wisdoms of Burford had been Lollards. In around 1530, a clothier from Burford called Simon Wisdom was charged with heresy by the Bishop of Lincoln. He owned illegal English translations of the four Gospels and of the Psalms. He also had a Protestant book called *The Sum of Holy*

Scripture, which had been condemned in 1530 for containing 'pestiferous errors and blasphemies'. Simon Wisdom survived his brush with the law, however, and in the 1540s was giving financial support to newly appointed clergy in Oxfordshire and Gloucestershire. What was the relationship (if any) between Simon and the other Wisdoms? Other than a shared interest in the textile business, we do not know; although it is tempting to think that Simon might have been Robert's father and John's elder brother.

If the family had a heretical past, it also had a Protestant future. John Wisdom's eldest son (and Gregory's brother), another John, drew up his will in November 1574, on his deathbed. Again, there was a fulsomely Protestant religious preamble, emphasizing his absolute trust in Christ's sacrifice. This was perhaps routine by 1574, but John went beyond mere lip service, ordering his executors to arrange and pay for six sermons to be preached in his parish church by 'some godly and learned man', the first of them at his own funeral. Similarly, when his widow Joan made her own will in 1576, she too proclaimed her Protestant faith and left money for 'some good honest preacher' to sermonize at her funeral. It was a classic Protestant gesture. It suggests a couple who were not only convinced Protestants, but who were part of the minority who called themselves 'godly' and whom others labelled 'Puritans'.

Did this family piety rub off on John's younger brother Gregory? It seems implausible. And yet, Gregory's own will, made twenty-five years later in 1599, also used fulsome and unambiguous Protestant phrasing. Perhaps that was no more than conventional by 1599, but the Wisdom family's thorough connections with Protestantism and religious reform make it credible. Nor is it the only evidence, as we shall see. Yet how could this be compatible with his activities as a magician?

To answer this question, we need to look more widely at how religion and magic regarded each other during this age of religious turmoil. Like most things involving Gregory Wisdom, the matter is murkier than it appears.

There is a well-established and well-grounded belief that Protestants hated magic.

Evidence for this hits us from every side. A good deal of what we know about the practice of magic in Tudor England comes from hostile Protestant witnesses. The fiercest broadside against magic fired in the whole century—certainly in England, possibly in Europe—was the work of a fervent Protestant gentleman from Kent named Reginald Scot. His 1584 book *The Discoverie of Witchcraft* was an exhaustive denial that magic of any kind was possible. A roll call of weighty Protestant theologians denounced magic in all its forms. One or two went so far as to write whole books on the subject; the attack on astrology written by John Calvin, the reformer of Geneva, was translated into English and published in 1561. Nor were these just paper protests. A series of Protestant bishops had their officials enquire in each parish whether anyone there used 'charms, sorcery, and enchantments, witchcraft, soothsaying, or any other wicked craft invented by the Devil'; so too did the royal visitation of the Church conducted in Edward VI's name in 1547. We know nothing—frustratingly—about how or why the 1542 Act against Conjurations came to be passed, but we do know that the 1563 Act against Conjurations, which replaced it, was supported enthusiastically in Parliament by Protestant hot-gospellers, and was enforced equally enthusiastically. Later in the century, a good many Protestants chafed at the way witchcraft was dealt with in English law: piecemeal, legalistically, and with a large number of acquittals. They looked enviously at Scotland or at Continental jurisdictions where witches could be hunted wholesale.

There were good theological reasons why Protestants should have loathed magic. Protestant theology stresses utter, childlike dependence on God, and worries that any attempt to find security or spiritual solace aside from God is blasphemy and idolatry. To this mindset, conjuring spirits can easily look like worshipping false gods. It scarcely mattered whether a magician thought he was conjuring angels or demons, because the New Testament warned that the Devil could masquerade as an angel of light. And workaday, popular magic could be condemned in the same breath: the Devil's power lay behind it all. Rather than appealing to magicians to solve their problems, good Christians should appeal to God in prayer. To Anthony Gilby, magic of any kind was 'spiritual fornication': strong words, but in Protestant eyes literally true, since those who should have been faithful to Christ alone were instead whoring after any dark powers that might help them.

Even the more respectable forms of magic were condemned. Astrology, in particular, attracted Protestant ire. A crude belief that the stars govern human destiny is of course quite incompatible with belief in a sovereign God; but Protestants also disliked the idea that God governed creation through the stars, or declared his purposes for the future in them. For even this seemed to suggest that God's freedom was constrained, or that he could not change his mind. Astrology, Protestants worried, engendered a certain fatalism. (The Calvinist doctrine of predestination which was the orthodoxy amongst English Protestants also had something of the same flavour to it—an irony which was not lost on astrology's defenders.) Numerous Protestants roundly denounced astrology, but perhaps the bluntest denial of it came from the radical John Hooper, later Bishop of Gloucester. Any kind of astrological prediction, he argued, was a blasphemy, because 'God hath not made the heavens to that end or purpose, that man should learn of them good fortune or ill.'

And yet, Hooper's attempt to discredit astrology led him onto very shaky ground. He attacked the medical use of astrology—which was near-universal, as we have seen—on the grounds that disease is caused by disobedience to God, not by the whim of the planets. But Hooper was too consistent a theologian not to follow his logic through. If the heavens could not cause illness, neither could earthbound influences. Neither corrupted air nor poisoned water could hurt a true Christian, he argued: 'but first man poisoneth himself with sin, and then God useth these elements ordained for the life of man to be the occasion of his death.' He observed that conventional wisdom for escaping the plague was to get out of town until the epidemic was over. But this, Hooper argued, was as blasphemous as astrology. For God had proclaimed that life and safety were to be found only in obeying his commandments. So, Hooper declared bravely, it did not matter if the air was filthy with the stench of plague, so long as

the conscience of a man in Christ be clean from sin. Though there die a thousand on the one side of thee, and ten thousand on the other side, thou shalt be safe.

This was a wonderfully demented piece of theology, magnificently consistent but maintaining only the most tenuous grasp on reality. (He covered himself by adding that, if a good Christian should happen to die of the plague, that was because God wished to ensure 'that no malice of the world should corrupt thy life'.) This argument—essentially, that cause and effect of any kind are an illusion—was so wildly implausible that none of the other opponents of astrology tried to repeat it. But they could not entirely escape its force. Roger

Hutchinson's 1550 attack on astrology argued, more subtly, that God permits normal causation, but is not constrained by it. As a result, however, he was forced to concede that the stars did have some predictive power. Calvin's treatise dealt with the whole issue much more convincingly, placing the stars firmly under the overarching providence of God: but he, too, was forced to concede that they had some real power over the earth.

The point of this is not just to watch theologians tying themselves in knots. Protestant theologians instinctively disliked magic in general, and astrology in particular, but they found it very difficult to mount *theological* arguments against it, as opposed to scientific ones. Their core argument—indeed, the main reason which Christians have used to oppose astrology from ancient times to the present—is a purely secular one: not that astrology was morally wrong, but simply that it didn't work. The punchiest sixteenth-century attack on the art, William Fulke's *Antiprognosticon*, took this view. The argument was of course embarrassingly strong. Fulke and others merely had to compare astrologers' predictions with what actually happened, then stand back and allow the art to collapse under the weight of its own errors. They could also mock the logic behind it. It was purely arbitrary, Fulke pointed out, to say that—for example—Saturn was a malevolent planet. Likewise, it was mere folly to delay treating a patient who obviously needed medical attention until the stars were correctly aligned. Others chipped in to ask why twins, born at the same moment, might have such different fates; or conversely, why thousands might perish together in battles or in natural disasters, sharing the same fate when they were all born under different stars.

Ridicule was the best weapon against the soothsayers. One of the very first astrological almanacs to survive in English is a spoof. In 1544 (the year when Gregory Wisdom met Lord Henry) this almanac informed readers solemnly, in its weather forecast for the year, that it would be windy:

> For men and women, when they have well dined
> Shall have no power to hold fast behind.
> The blasts shall be boisterous, big and outrageous;
> Wherefore the air must needs be contagious.

And it warned that

> If the ninth day of November
> Had fallen upon tenth day of December
> It had been a marvellous hot year for bees
> For then had the Moon been like a green cheese.

This sort of thing was good clean(ish) fun, and could probably do more to discredit astrology than any weighty tract, but it was hardly a theological point.

As it happens, there was a theological reason why Protestants hated astrology and magic of all kinds. But it was not a particularly respectable or compelling reason. That reason was that they wanted to associate magic with Catholicism: to damn each by association with the other. From the very beginning of the Reformation, we find Protestants claiming that Catholicism is simply a kind of witchcraft, and that Catholic priests were (as one preacher put it) 'the vilest witches and sorcerers of the earth'. The scurrilous Protestant pamphleteer and playwright John Bale led the charge. It was apparently Bale who first used the derogatory term *priestcraft* to describe Catholicism, suggesting a parallel to witchcraft. He alleged that the Mass was the central rite of all ceremonial magic: 'it serveth all witches in their witchery, all sorcerers, charmers, enchanters, dreamers, soothsayers, necromancers, conjurers, cross-diggers, devil-raisers,

miracle-doers, dog-leeches and bawds. For without a Mass,
they cannot well work their feats.' In his play the *Comedy
Concerning Three Laws*, he presented the Catholic character
Idolatry as a witch, whose piety in saying her traditional Latin
prayers was 'revealed' to be mere sorcery:

> She can by saying her *Ave Mary*,
> And by other charms of sorcery,
> Ease men of toothache by and by,
> Yea, and fetch the Devil from Hell.

But Bale was only one of a crowd of Protestants hurling similar allegations. One wrote in the late 1540s that conjurers were
actually less diabolical than Catholics: for the former merely
try to conjure spirits into a crystal, while the latter try to
conjure Christ himself into a piece of bread at the Mass, using
the words *Hoc est corpus meum*—the words of consecration.
Indeed, the seventeenth-century term *hocus-pocus* may well
have been a parody of those very words, reducing them to
mere magical mumbo-jumbo. And while these attacks were
clearly malicious, they had some real force. The Catholic
liturgy might be theologically correct, but its being in Latin
naturally gave it the air of an invocation.

Moreover, Catholics really did claim to be able to work
miracles. Most Protestants believed that the age of miracles
had ceased, but part of Catholicism's appeal was the prospect
that God might still perform wonders for believers: healings,
exorcisms, visions. To Protestants, this sounded very like the
magicians' boasts. It also, damagingly, laid the old Church
open to claims of systematic fraud, because every so often
faked miracles came to light. In 1538, a life-size crucifix at
Boxley in Kent was discovered to contain the rusted remnants
of a mechanism which (so zealous Protestants concluded) had
been used to make its eyes and limbs move, in an attempt to

hoodwink credulous pilgrims into believing they had seen a miracle. It was taken to London and triumphantly displayed to the people as hard proof of Catholic trickery, and became notorious.

Alongside this kind of debunking sat more disturbing legends, of Catholic priests who had not merely faked magic, but actually conjured spirits and bargained with the Devil. Several popes were said to have been necromancers. Sylvester II was pope in the year 1000, when (some Protestants argued) he had set the Devil free from his long captivity. The name of Pope Honorius III had also long been attached to one of the more openly blasphemous texts of black magic. It was said that Cardinal Morton, Henry VII's tough-minded chief minister, had had a licence from the Pope to study necromancy; and that Cardinal Wolsey had used his own skills as a sorcerer to befuddle Henry VIII. St Dunstan of Canterbury was traditionally said to have seized the Devil by the nose with red-hot tongs: Protestants claimed that the two of them had had a rather more cordial relationship.

This claim—that Catholicism was a form of sorcery— was very widespread. It was even true, in two very limited senses. First, some Catholics, indeed some Catholic clergy and perhaps even the occasional pope, were magical enthusiasts. Second, a good deal of magic piggy-backed on Catholic rites and sacred objects. Magical texts like the one attributed to Pope Honorius included rituals which were clearly perversions of Catholicism, and which used Catholicism as an arsenal of sacred power. The problem (for the Protestants) was that most Catholics were thoroughly outraged by this. So far from defending magic, Catholics competed with Protestants to denounce it. When Queen Mary restored Catholicism in England in 1553–4, her bishops continued to enquire after popular magical practices just as their Protestant predecessors had (indeed, using precisely the same wording). Edmund Bonner, the Bishop of London who had arrested Robert Wisdom in 1541 and who enthusiastically enforced the Catholic restoration in the 1550s, violently denounced those 'that do use witchcraft, Necromancy, enchantment, or any other such like ungodly, and superstitious trade, or have any confidence in such things'—singling out those who used demons to find hidden treasure. Perhaps these expostulations were partly a reaction to Protestant accusations, but magicians of all kinds had been troubled by Catholic authorities long before the Reformation. One of the most popular English Catholic devotional manuals of the pre-Reformation period, Richard Whitford's *A work for householders*, fulminated against magic very much as his Protestant successors would. Magic was, he warned, a form of idolatry. Magicians and cunningfolk were 'the Devil's proctors', and in the unlikely event that they ever did what they claimed to be able to do, it was either through deceit or 'the Devil's craft'.

As things turned out, the Catholic voices were shouted down. The Protestants' claim that their religion was the very opposite of magic, but that Catholicism was deeply implicated in it, has been remarkably tenacious. Especially since the eighteenth century, Protestantism has claimed to be the liberal, modernizing, rational form of Christianity (Catholicism, of course, is the superstitious, obscurantist form). According to this myth, Protestants were the precursors of scientific rationalism, sceptical of magic in all its forms. Indeed, they were also the forefathers of modern capitalism, of liberal democracy, of tolerant pluralism, and, indeed, of the modern world in general. This is a powerful and enduring myth, enduring not least because it has a fair amount of truth in it. But it *is* a myth. Specifically, it is a 'just-so story', a tale which starts from the modern world and works backwards, conscripting history to tell us what we want to hear rather than letting the past explain itself. It is a myth which writes out inconvenient elements of the story (elements such as the Wisdoms). If we can keep our grubby twenty-first-century hands off early Protestantism, and let it be itself, then it might be able to tell us something not only about the sixteenth century but (if we are lucky) our own.

In reality, English Protestants were not nearly so firmly opposed to magic as they would have liked to think.

Some of them, as we have seen, affected a rationalist scepticism towards magic. But this was a good deal harder in the sixteenth century than it would be today, since so much of the best learning of the age suggested that magic of some kinds was possible. Often the sceptics look like ignorant scoffers: like modern doubters using 'common sense' and incredulity to argue that evolution is false, that the Moon landings were a fraud, or that the Earth is flat. The more intelligent and sophisticated writers knew that it was easier to ridicule magic than to argue it away. In particular, 'natural magic' (that slippery category) and astrology had powerful scientific arguments in their favour. But a well-read, open-minded scholar in the sixteenth century would have found it difficult to dismiss almost any form of magic entirely.

Indeed, one stance on magic—taken by both Protestants and Catholics—was to acknowledge its reality at the same time as condemning it. This was in some ways a much more honourable position than rationalist mockery. It is easy to forbid magic if you think it does not work. To admit its power, and then forswear it on moral grounds, is altogether more costly. Yet this was common enough. William Tyndale, the Bible translator, admitted that magicians and soothsayers could sometimes make accurate predictions: but he added,

'What then? God wills that we care not to know what shall come. He will have us care only to keep his commandments.' Anthony Gilby agreed that the sorcerers whom he condemned really could have access to limitless knowledge, 'if it please your great master the Devil'. John Jewel, the Bishop of Salisbury, admitted that conjurers truly could command demons, if they were willing to mortgage themselves to yet more powerful demons. Roger Hutchinson, writing in 1550, attacked those sceptics who thought that the Devil was simply a metaphor:

> I send them to conjurers, sorcerers, enchanters, charmers, witches; which will learn and persuade them that there be devils, and that they be not lusts of the flesh, but spiritual substances and spirits created for vengeance.

The Protestant surgeon John Hall, writing early in Elizabeth's reign, even cited Girolamo Cardano, whom we have already met as a physician, mathematician, and astrologer (see p. 123). Cardano, Hall noted, believed that some illnesses were caused by 'enchantment, or the working of cursed sciences'. Hall accepted this, but violently disputed Cardano's conclusion, which was that sufferers from these illnesses had no choice but to defend themselves with counter-magic. Christians, Hall insisted, should never resort to devils for any reason whatsoever; instead, they should simply suffer and pray. The only solution he could offer to the luckless Protestant victim of sorcery was to enforce the law against witches. 'If none such (as God in his holy law hath commanded), were suffered to live,' the problem would not arise.

This was a grimly austere viewpoint (not to say homicidal). To admit the power and even the necessity of magic, but to refuse to use it: it is admirable in its own way, but it must have seemed quixotic at the time. Those suffering from what they suspected were magical ailments, or in desperate need of magical assistance, would surely hear the affirmation of magic's power more readily than the warnings against it. And indeed, Hall fretted that Protestants were as enthusiastic as Catholics in seeking out 'devilish witches and sorcerers, if their finger do but ache'. Given his own testimony to those sorcerers' powers, he should not have been surprised.

On astrology, the Protestant witness was even more ambiguous. Almost all of those who wrote against the art also admitted that it had its legitimate uses, and some of these concessions were pretty far-reaching. John Hall may have given no quarter to enchantment, but he (like most physicians) thought astrology was a necessary branch of medicine. In his attack on popular soothsayers, he mocked a man who professed to be an astrologer but who was unable to give coherent answers when questioned by a *real* astrologer. Lawrence Humphrey, whom we have already met denouncing the nobility's unhealthy interest in astrology, admitted that the art was a valuable guide to knowing oneself and to governing household and nation. The mathematician Edward Worsop was fierce in condemning 'divinatory and judicial astrology'. But the authorities he cited against it included Cornelius Agrippa and even his own contemporary John Dee. Astrology, Worsop argued, was based on a scientific reality. 'Philosophy,' he wrote, 'proveth sundry influences, proceeding from the celestial bodies, to the terrestrial.'

Nowadays we would disagree, but this was the cutting edge of sixteenth-century learning. Philip Melanchthon, the brilliant liberal philosopher–theologian of Lutheranism, was well known as a moderate defender of astrology. Even John Calvin insisted that 'the science of Astrology is honourable', because 'all creatures which are under heaven are subject to the order of heaven, to draw from it some qualities'. He accepted the medical use of the art, and the connection between the alignment of the stars and 'the disposition of man's body'. He also believed that astrological influences partly determined personality, although he doubted that this influence could be pinned down with any precision. On a larger scale, he accepted that the stars caused not only the weather, but

> barrenness and pestilences. . . . We see an order and, as it were, a knot and tying together of the things which are above with the things that are beneath. . . . One may seek in the heavenly creatures the beginning and cause of the accidents which are sent here in the earth.

Plenty of Protestants took him at his word, and embraced astrology enthusiastically. Miles Coverdale, one of the heroes of the early English Reformation, produced a Protestantized astrological almanac in 1535, based on a German original. This denounced the belief that the stars have any independent power, while accepting that God uses them to show his purposes. The almanac's predictions were entirely based on the Bible, and were conventionally preacherly; but he claimed to be practising 'theological astronomy' and even praised the Old Testament prophet Amos as 'a certain true astronomer'. Perhaps Coverdale was subverting astrology, but he was hardly attacking it.

Later Protestants were even more forthright. We have already met John Cheke and Thomas Smith, two of mid-Tudor England's most brilliant scholars, both earnest Protestants and earnest astrologers (see pp. 123–4). Leonard Digges was an accomplished mathematician whose Protestantism nearly cost him his life in Queen Mary's reign; he robustly defended astrology. William Cunningham, the physician who witnessed John Wisdom's will in 1559, published an almanac every year: on occasion these included

unambiguously Protestant calls to repentance, alongside predictions of epidemics and of political events. And indeed, the
mass of almanacs which poured from the printing presses of
post-Reformation England were steadily Protestant in their
flavour, sometimes (by the time of the civil wars of the 1640s)
violently so. The theologians' hesitations were swept away by
an apparently insatiable popular Protestant hunger for astrological guidance.

This kind of astrology did have a kind of threadbare
respectability, but some Protestants were more deeply implicated. The Scottish Protestant nobleman Sir John Borthwick,
who spent much of the 1530s and 1540s in England, was
an enthusiast for astrological prophecies, and described how
he had tried to use an 'astrolok'—apparently an instrument
of some kind—to predict the future politics of Scotland,
Denmark, Germany, and Italy. When the German Lutheran
physician–astrologer Eliseus Bomelius came to England in
the 1560s, he was surrounded by a cluster of admiring Protestant grandees. John Bale, the scourge of Catholic magic, was
his close friend; the Puritan Bishop of London, Edmund
Grindal, authorized one of his almanacs. He may even have
done astrological work for Queen Elizabeth. Yet Bomelius'
astrology was hardly tame. He apparently built up a considerable reputation for himself in England as a prophet,
even while he was close to the government's counsels. He
eventually took himself to Russia, where he became a court
magician to Ivan the Terrible and offered his new master a
series of enticing prophecies. This was a foolish game, and it
ended with Bomelius dying in the tsar's prisons; but he died
still firmly and apparently sincerely professing his Protestant
faith. Good Protestants at court should not perhaps have been
involved with such a man, but as we know (see p. 144), back in
1549, good Protestants at court had hired the conjurer William

Wycherley to find lost property for them with a spirit in a crystal.

An anecdote told by a Scottish Protestant can perhaps sum up the whole mess. In around 1550, James Melville of Halhill was in France, and came across a young man named Taggot, whom he described (ominously) as a great scholar of mathematics. Taggot's researches had contained a nasty surprise for himself. He had discovered 'by the art of palmistry' that he would die before he reached the age of twenty-eight. Apparently reconciled to this fate, he told Melville that 'I know the true religion to be exercised at Geneva; there will I go and end in God's service.' And indeed, Melville added, Taggot died in the Calvinist city of Lausanne, at the time forecast. Calvin and the Genevans would hardly have approved. Palmistry was superstition, and any belief in an irrevocable fate was an insult to God's sovereignty. Yet Taggot apparently saw no contradiction. Indeed, it was the knowledge of his own impending death which led him to put his religious affairs in order. This kind of magical–Protestant eclecticism may not have made much theological sense. But clearly that did not prevent it having an appeal.

So much for what the voices of religious authority had to say about magic. The picture is different again when we look at the other side, at the magicians themselves.

Some of the more excitable Protestant (and Catholic) accusations against magicians are obviously untrue. There is very little real evidence that these people consciously and deliberately believed themselves to be serving the Devil. The legend of the Faustian pact is, indeed, a legend. Obviously enough: for who, believing in the existence of a Devil and of an eternal Hell, would deliberately condemn himself to that Hell for any price? The few instances of real, historical Faustian pacts were more ambiguous and conditional than the legend allows: the bargainers hoped to escape the Devil's clutches. In 1596 a hapless young student at the German Lutheran university of Tübingen was arrested for making a Faustian pact. Under examination, the full story came out. The lad had been desperate to clear his debts. Like all teenagers, he was confident of his own health and longevity: so he proposed to lease his soul to the Devil, rather than sell it outright. The terms of the deal were that he would have been damned if, and only if, he had died within two years of making the pact. He also told the university authorities that he had intended to cheat the Devil by repenting even if he had died within the two years. This did not prevent them from taking a dim view of his actions.

Perhaps there were a handful of atheists (if *atheist* was a word with any real meaning in early modern Europe) or of genuine Devil-worshippers in the sixteenth century. Possibly the real Johannes Faustus, if he even existed, belonged in one or both of these categories. He remains a mysterious and sinister figure, hidden beneath layers of encrusted legend. But all magicians were baptized Christians or circumcised Jews, and while their view of their faiths may not have been wholly orthodox, the evidence is that most of them took their religion seriously. Indeed, they saw their magic as a natural outgrowth from their religion; appealing to the same powers, perhaps in very similar words and rituals, but simply for more practical reasons. Judaism and Christianity provided sets of holy words, objects, places, times, and ideas which could be used to gain access to supernatural power. If magicians did so, that may have made them bad, or unorthodox Jews or Christians: but unless they were in some sense Jews or Christians, they would hardly have tried at all.

The most widespread evidence for this is the extensive use of Christian prayers as magical invocations, which Protestant

propagandists so detested. Solomonic magic of all kinds
revolved around the use of the names of God or of the
angels. Sometimes it is genuinely hard to tell whether this
was incantation or prayer. William Byg was arrested for conjuring spirits in 1467: his technique was to say aloud the
three Latin prayers which most good Catholics knew by heart
(the Paternoster, the Ave Maria, and the Apostles' Creed),
adding a prayer to Christ to send angels who could answer his
questions. When the angels appeared, he would charge them
to tell him the truth in the name of God and of the Virgin
Mary. The Church profoundly disliked this sort of thing, but
it was hardly un-Christian.

If we turn to the magicians' books themselves, the evidence is even clearer. Grimoires, or magical manuals, did
not only take fragments of Jewish or Christian ritual and
use them for their own purposes. Some show real signs of
actual piety. And in some cases, that piety appears to be
Protestant, or at least post-Reformation, in its flavour. Take,
for example, the enterprising astrologer–magician whom we
met in Chapter 4 experimenting on his own daughter (see
p. 117). His technique for invoking spirits used the names of
archangels, of Christ, and of the Trinity—as was common—
but also betrayed some distinctively Protestant scruples. To
summon angels when it was not necessary, he warned,
was to reject 'God's offered grace and providence' and to
plunge into a 'diabolical labyrinth of superstition and im-
pious idolatry'. In particular, if you did summon an angel,
you must not commit idolatry by reverencing or worshipping it: and he cited a passage from the Book of Revela-
tion which forbade doing just that. The danger of implicitly
rejecting God's grace, the importance of his providence, and
above all the loathing of idolatry were all classic Protestant
concerns.

Or again, consider an Elizabethan grimoire which sits squarely in the Solomonic tradition, and includes instructions on how to conjure a range of spirits ranging from Oberon, King of the Fairies, to Satan himself (of whom the author helpfully provided a pen-and-ink sketch). Yet this piece also begins with a very lengthy prayer praising God for his mercy on his unworthy people, only slowly settling onto his particular mercy in providing the wisdom and knowledge necessary to conjure spirits. It carefully acknowledges that the magician's authority over the spirits can only be God-given. And mixed in with its rituals, apparently indiscriminately, are a pair of English-language texts cited in the new Protestant translations: the first chapter of St John's Gospel, and the

14. Pen-and-ink sketch of Satan taken from an Elizabethan grimoire.

Athanasian Creed. Both of these have the kind of rhythmic, holy obscurity which might suit a magician, but they were nevertheless mainstream post-Reformation Christian texts. And as we have seen, much the same is true of the *Dannel*, the grimoire which John and Gregory Wisdom themselves may have owned. Its rituals too begin with a prayer exculpating the magician from any sin in the conjuring of spirits, and acknowledging God's sovereignty over the whole process.

From an orthodox Protestant (or Catholic) point of view, this was of course foul self-deception of the most damnable kind. If magicians thought their practices were acceptable, or even pious, they were desperately deluded. But we might ask, how did they come to embrace such a delusion? In particular, when Protestant clergy thundered so relentlessly against magic, how on earth could otherwise intelligent men and women believe that they could be both Protestants and magicians? This was a question which most of those clergy avoided, but John Calvin, the most limpidly brilliant of them, asked it, and his answer is worth listening to despite its vehemence.

Calvin's worry was that a great many people converted to Protestantism out of impure motives. Instead of love for God and a desire for true learning, he claimed, what drove these false gospellers was the wish to 'have something to talk upon in company', to 'seek their own gain; yea, and there be some that abuse it to practise bawdry thereby, to get access to their women and ladies'. Others have no understanding of the Protestant gospel at all, but 'they are ashamed to see others take hold upon it, and that they should be despised by their ignorance'. The result was that almost all turned the true doctrine of salvation into 'a certain profane philosophy'. As such, it was no surprise that they also turned to magic. Indeed, for this reason, Calvin believed that belief in magic was becoming ever more widespread, with most of the growth coming from Protestants. From his point of view, it was a just punishment from God: false Christians were being allowed to fall into further folly.

Leaving aside the judgemental tone, this is not a bad analysis. No doubt for many converts a part of the appeal of Protestantism was the doctrine of salvation it taught, but for others, it seems clear, it had other attractions. Some of these were venal: it was new, exciting, radical, a fashion to be followed. Other attractions ran deeper: the new gospel did indeed offer a new philosophy, profane or otherwise. By encouraging converts to throw off the mental disciplines of Catholicism, the new gospel opened up new intellectual vistas. As G. K. Chesterton might have said, the first effect of not believing in Catholicism was not to believe in Protestantism, but to believe in anything.

Certainly this is the impression we get from some of those newly enamoured by magical ideas. Not many people in England knew much about the Renaissance magi, but they did know that the Renaissance was opening up new worlds of the mind, and that abandoning the constraints of Catholicism was a part of that process. The Protestant mathematician Edward Worsop believed that 'in the time of popery most singular knowledges were shut up', and that 'pure Mathematical knowledges' had only begun to flourish since the papal yoke had been lifted—and as we have seen, *mathematics* could be a loaded term. William Cunningham, the Protestant astrologer who witnessed John Wisdom's will, was likewise an enthusiast for the most up-to-date, world-changing science. He boasted that his astrological calculations drew on the work of Copernicus, the Polish astronomer who had recently made the revolutionary argument that the earth revolved around the sun, not vice versa. (Needless to say, Copernicus' views in part reflected his own mystical convictions about the sun's spiritual centrality.) Cunningham also celebrated the explorers of his own age who had discovered the Americas (as so often, Columbus was forgotten and Amerigo Vespucci given the glory). The explorers were, Cunningham wrote, bringing to light a world far larger and wilder than had ever been suspected. He described dragons, cockatrices, unicorns, and men with dogs' heads, alongside such equally fabulous sights such as elephants, tigers, camels, and pygmies. There were new skies, too: Cunningham knew enough about the strange stars of the southern hemisphere to describe the Southern Cross.

In such an alien, exhilarating new world, even the most level-headed intellects could become intoxicated by possibility. In our own age, scepticism and disbelief seem intellectually sophisticated; in the sixteenth century, they seemed self-limiting and perverse. It was unmistakable that there were more things in heaven and earth than had been dreamed of in the old philosophies. Credulity, or at least a willingness to believe, was the only sensible way of looking at the world. And when you have adopted a new mathematics, a new astronomy, a new geography and a new religion, why balk at a new magic?

It is time to return to the Wisdoms. For it appears that Gregory Wisdom and Henry, Lord Neville may also have been caught up in this ferment of novelty.

As usual, it is Lord Henry's stance which is the clearer. Because Lord Henry's son Charles was to lead a rebellion against Queen Elizabeth in the name of Catholicism, he himself has often been assumed to be a Catholic, or at least a religious conservative. In fact, what evidence there is seems to point the other way. During Queen Mary's Catholic restoration, the organizers of the one of the conspiracies against her thought that Lord Henry (by then the earl of Westmorland)

might support them. They were probably wrong, but this
at least indicates that he had a reputation as a Protestant
sympathizer. Once Elizabeth became queen, Henry certainly
set about enforcing her new Protestant settlement with a will.
Back in the mid-1540s, from time of his arrest, there are
rather clearer signs. The two men whom he met for Christmas Day gambling in 1544, Sir Nicholas Poyntz and Robert
Thistlethwayt, were both Protestant fellow-travellers. This,
apparently, was Lord Henry's social circle. And when he was
imprisoned in 1546, writing to Sir William Paget to beg for his
life, he filled his letters with Protestant phrases, buzzwords,
and ideas. This may have been disingenuous: Paget too had
a reputation for being a Protestant sympathizer, and Lord
Henry may merely have been trying to ingratiate himself.
But it is equally plausible that he had picked up on the
reformism which was becoming fashionable amongst young
courtiers. He claimed to Paget that he had professed God's
Word with his lips yet dishonoured it with his deeds, which
suggests more than mere dissimulation. At the very least, he
showed a striking familiarity with the jargon and catchphrases
of Protestantism.

And now this leads us back to the very heart of Lord Henry
and Wisdom's plot. When Wisdom offered to murder Lord
Henry's wife, he did not simply point out how Lord Henry
would benefit: he also presented a theological argument to
justify what he was proposing. Lord Henry protested that
murder was a sin, but Wisdom had a less simplistic view of
the matter. As Lord Henry remembered it, Wisdom said:

> I know that she (the good lady) would wish to be dead, and
> I know her soul shall be saved. Therefore it [the murder]
> shall be her salvation, and a way to make you God's ser-
> vant.... You may choose you a wife that you can love, where
> the life that you lead now shall destroy both your body and
> soul.

Lord Henry claimed to have found this oddly persuasive. Persuading Lord Henry may not have been the hardest job in Tudor England, but this is an argument which could be made to fit with the new Protestant approach to personal morality. Not (of course) that Protestants believed in murder, but they did believe that committing a single, isolated sin was less damaging than living a life steeped in sin. In place of the old Catholic pattern—where each sin individually had to be confessed and atoned for—Protestants argued for a new start, a thorough regeneration of life. This was what Wisdom was offering: 'a way to make you God's servant'.

Of course, orthodox Protestant doctrine said that you become regenerate through the grace of God rather than by killing your wife. Yet Protestants also argued that sins (such as, for example, killing your wife) would be freely forgiven by God. The old demand that penance should be done was abandoned as detracting from divine grace. Faith alone was all that was needed for salvation. Catholics were outraged by this: they claimed that by offering free forgiveness in this way, Protestants were giving people a licence to sin without fear of the consequences. It was an unfair accusation, which misrepresented Protestant theology. Protestant theologians took sin extremely seriously, and did not really believe that you could sin with impunity. But if you *wanted* to sin with impunity; or if you were in a situation where a single sin (however grave) would be all it took to break you out of an otherwise inescapable cycle of self-destruction . . . well, then the Protestant approach could seem terribly appealing.

So, was Gregory Wisdom a godly Protestant? Of course not. He was a liar, a thief, a conjurer, and (probably in earnest) a would-be murderer. Likewise, Lord Henry was hardly a paragon of the new religious virtues. But they both lived and moved in worlds where Protestant ideas and conviction were widespread, and where Protestant jargon and assumptions had become commonplace. And most Protestants were not exemplary Protestants, any more than most Catholics were exemplary Catholics. As Calvin recognized, all sorts of people ended up being associated with the Protestant cause one way or another. In particular, magical ideas and practices were woven into the social fabric of the new faith. The theologians had hoped that their Reformation would purge such godless practices from Christendom. Instead, it appears that they adapted and flourished.

This, then, is Gregory Wisdom's story of the Reformation in England. That Reformation did not make England into a nation of godly Protestants, or anything like it. What it did do was shatter religious and intellectual certainty. It hacked English culture free of its moorings, so that religious and intellectual identities were up for grabs. In the reign of Henry VIII, English people (or at least the social elites) were forced to make choices about who they were, choices none of their ancestors had had to make for a thousand years. And those choices were complicated. It was not a simple matter of Catholic versus Protestant (partly because no one quite knew what those terms meant yet). There were suddenly dozens of overlapping, competing, and complementary identities on offer: papist, gospeller, Anabaptist, humanist, astrologer, mathematician, magician. The apparent spike of interest in magic of all kinds (and the moral panic which it triggered) cannot be separated from the religious upheaval. Much as the Protestants disliked magic, their movement created the intellectual space in which magic could flourish. Gregory Wisdom's Reformation, Lord Henry's Reformation, was not about making Catholics into Protestants, or making modernity out of medievalism. It was not about the rise of rationality or tolerance. It was about chaos: bewildering, exciting, fruitful, contradictory, and sometimes murderous intellectual chaos. It was a process of shattering a religious community into shards, some of which flew in unpredictable directions. It produced a world which may seem familiar to modern eyes: one in which astrology, Solomon, or Orpheus were as credible as the Catholic Mass or the Protestant gospel, and in which beliefs and world views were readily rebuilt according to need, to preference, or (in particular) to profit.

Conclusion

Barbarians at the Gates

GREGORY Wisdom has taken most of his secrets with him. Most of what we think we know about him is uncertain. We have the bare bones of biographical outline and family history, and a few snapshots of other incidents. These are not enough to tell his life story, and I have not tried to do so. Instead, I have used those fragments to try to conjure up the world, or the worlds, he lived in: civic, medical, noble, criminal, magical, religious. As with most conjuring tricks, the resulting pictures are to some extent an illusion. I hope I have not piled conjecture too high, but this is a game with few certainties. Often we do not have Wisdom's footprints to place him firmly at the scene of the crime: merely an echo of his steps and of that smoothly persuasive voice.

What we are left with is what we started with: a story. It is a timeless story of a hustler and his victim: a fool and his money. But it is also a story very much of its time. This was a febrile moment in English history when new opportunities and new worlds were opening up. Some of those openings were created by established social, religious, and political elites. Yet it was not the elites who poured through these gaps and took advantage of them in new ways. Instead, those elites found themselves struggling to contain what they had unleashed. The old nobility battled for their places in a world where low-born bureaucrats seemed to have taken charge. The medical establishment fought to keep the 'empirics' out in the cold.

London's city fathers wrestled to control a city whose population was rocketing, and where they feared—not entirely without reason—that a swelling underclass was coalescing into an organized underworld. Learned opinion of all kinds tried to insulate itself from the dangerously alluring fashion for occult knowledge, even as that knowledge drew some of its support from the best modern scholarship. The old Catholic establishment, mortally wounded by Henry VIII, fought bitterly to keep down the Protestant heretics. And the Protestants, those earnest and high-minded idealists who aspired to be the new religious establishment themselves, strove to ostracize the magical practices and other heterodoxies which their own revolt had set free.

In the end, the establishments won most of these battles. The nobility were edged aside and the old Church was suppressed: but new governing and religious elites replaced them and reasserted their control with verve. By the time of Gregory Wisdom's death in 1599, a newly systematic approach to relieving poverty and policing criminality was beginning to take hold. The medical establishment's grip was tightening and religious orthodoxies were being enforced vigorously by an increasingly confident Protestant church. When the elites' control was challenged again in the civil wars of the 1640s, it broke along different lines.

But that mid-sixteenth-century moment of flux had its consequences. Henry VIII, the most absolute and tyrannical king in English history, presided over social fractures which ensured that none of his successors could ever wield the same kind of authority. If the elites retained their power, it was only through sharing that power with wider circles than ever before. Some of the poachers had to be allowed to become gamekeepers. It was a pattern that would become familiar in English life over the following centuries.

One such poacher was Gregory Wisdom. This young artisan painter-stainer, probably only a first- or second-generation Londoner, first put together a living for himself as a dealer in fine fabrics. He then followed his father's illicit surgical practice and probably also followed his father in becoming a self-educated magician. He and his family aligned themselves early with the rising Protestant establishment, an alignment which only reinforced his magical learning despite that establishment's horror of the occult. When the pair of them won a stunning victory by having their medical status legitimized, the young man used that status to inveigle himself into gentry and noble households, weaving an aura of medical and magical knowledge about himself to swindle his patrons out of substantial amounts of cash. He seems to have done this in part through maintaining and exploiting his contacts in the criminal underworld. He was slippery or lucky enough to avoid being trapped by these contradictions. And when he finally paid (handsomely) for formal admission to the medical establishment, the transition was complete. The elites had now reasserted their authority over the likes of him: so he became one of them, a respectable elderly physician of impeccably godly family. His scandals were long since buried in the archives. Perhaps he had become a reformed character; perhaps he had simply learned to be cautious enough not to leave any traces. As usual, he will not tell us. All we can do is acknowledge the scale of the transformation he wrought in himself. Whether it was real or an illusion, it was his greatest conjuring trick.

Appendix

Gregory Wisdom's Will: Guildhall Library, London, MS 9051/5 fos. 139v–141r

I N dei nomine Amen. The three and twentieth day of September Anno domini 1599 and in the one and fortieth year of the reign of our sovereign lady Elizabeth, by the grace of God Queen of England France and Ireland Defender of the faith etc., I Gregory Wisdom of London, Practitioner of physic, weak in body but of good and perfect mind and memory (thanked be Almighty god) weighing and considering with myself the instability of this transitory life, the certainty of death, and the uncertain time when and where the same shall approach, for the quiet of my mind and discharge of my conscience do make, ordain and declare this my present last will and Testament in manner and form following, viz.

First and before all thinges I commit commend and bequeath my soul into the hands of Almighty God the Father son and holy ghost three persons in Trinity, and one God in unity; trusting most assuredly to be saved, and to inherit the kingdom of heaven, by and through the only merits death passion resurrection and ascension of my only Lord and Saviour Christ Jesu. My body I commit to the earth from whence it came, to be decently buried according to the good discretions of my Executors hereafter named.

Gregory Wisdom's will, as recorded in the City of London's probate register.

140

ffirst and before all thinges I comitt rennder and bequeath
my soule into the handes of Allmyghtie the ffather sonne &
holie ghoste thre psons in Trinity, and one God in vnity
trusting most assuredly to be saved, and to inherit the kingi=
dome of heaven, by and through the onlie meritts deathe
passion resurrection and ascention of my onlie Lorde and
Saviour Christ Jesu. my bodye I comitt to the earth
from whence it came, to be decently buried according to the
good discretions of my Executors hereafter named Item I
geve and bequeath to and amonge the poore howsholders within
the parish of St miracles in Battersham London the somme
of fforty shillinges to be distributed vnto them the daie of my buri=
all Item I geve and bequeath to my cosen Anne Brodehate
widdowe and to John Brodbent her sonne to either of them
Twenty shillinges in golde to make either of them a ringe Item
I geve and bequeath to my cosen Abell Allen twenty
shillinges in golde to make him a ringe Item I geve and
bequeath to Anne Walker wiffe of ____ Walker Twenty
shillinges in golde to make her a ringe Item I geve and bequeath
to my antient and trustie servant Joseph Burke all my
right title interest terme of yeares yet to come and demaund
wch I have or ought to have of or in the littell tenement within
the Savoy now in the tenure of widow Ainsworth beinge
percell of my lease therewth I have of the master and
Chapleins of the saide Savoy, to have holde and enioye
the said littell tenement for and duringe the residue of the
yeares yet to come in the same And further my will and
minde is that my said Executors hereafter named
shall geve and bestowe vppon my said servant Joseph
Burke of the moneye cominge of my said lease the somme
of ten poundes Item I geve and bequeath to my cosen
Richard Allen Clarke twenty shillings in gold to make
him a ringe Item I geve and bequeath to Agnes Mayers
one Ale silver pott wth out yeare wayinge about fc—
ounces And for that I have had good experience of the
care and kindnes of my good friend mr wm Hutchinson
doctor of divinity John Stover Baker and John
Humfrey Clotheworker And for that I knowe not how
without the labour and friendshipp of them the said william
Hutchinson John Stover and John Humfrey above
named my goods and chattells wilbe made liable to beare
the charges of this & my will devise Allndnall I therfore
the residue of all my goods chattells and leases whatsoever
(if any be) shalbe and remaine to my said good friend
william Hutchinson John Stover and John Humfrey
to

15. (*Continued*)

15. *(Continued)*

141

Item I give and bequeath to and among the poor house-holders within the parish of St Michaels in Bassishaw, London, the sum of forty shillings to be distributed unto them the day of my burial. Item I give and bequeath to my cousins Anne Broadbent, widow, and to John Broadbent her son, to either of them Twenty shillings in gold to make either of them a ring. Item I give and bequeath to my cousin Abell Allen twenty shillings in gold to make him a ring. Item I give bequeath to Anne Walker wife of   Walker Twenty shillings in gold to make her a ring. Item I give bequeath to my ancient and trusty servant Joseph Bucke all my right title, interest, term of years yet to come, and demand which I have or ought to have of or in the title Tenement within the Savoy now in the tenure of widow Aynsworth, being parcel of my lease there which I have of the Master and Chaplains of the said Savoy, to have hold and enjoy the said little Tenement for and during the residue of the years yet to come in the same. And further my will and mind is that my said Executors hereafter named shall give and bestow upon my said servant Joseph Bucke, of the money coming of my foresaid lease, the sum of Ten pounds.

Item I give and bequeath to my cousin Richard Allen, clerk, twenty shillings in gold to make him a ring. Item I give and bequeath to Agnes Hayes one little silver pot with one ear weighing about six ounces. And for that I have had good experience of the care and kindness of my good friends master William Hutchinson doctor of divinity, John Storer baker, and John Humfrey clothworker, and for that I know not how (without the labour and friendship of them the said William Hutchinson John Storer and John Humfrey above named) my goods and chattels will be made able to bear the charges of this my will devices and funeral; therefore the residue of all my goods chattels and leases whatsoever (if any be) shall be and remain to my said good friends William Hutchinson, John Storer and John Humfrey to their own proper uses and behoofs for ever, to do and dispose therewith as they shall think best. And I do make and constitute the said William Hutchinson, John Storer and John Humfrey Executors of this my last will and Testament. And hereby I do renounce and annihilate all other my former wills whatsoever. In witness whereof to this my present last will and Testament, I, the said Gregory Wisdom, have put my hand and seal, given the said three and Twentieth day of September in the one and fortieth year of the reign of our said Sovereign Lady Queen Elizabeth aforesaid.

Witnesses: Richard Gyle, Richard Graye and John Flemynge (Flemynge only making his mark).

Notes

CHAPTER 1

The key papers relating to Lord Henry's case are in the National Archives [hereafter NA], SP 1/226, fos. 119–31. The main narrative account of the case, which this chapter follows, is at fos. 119–22. Other key documents are at SP 1/225 fos. 115, 125. All of these documents are summarized in *Letters and Papers, Foreign and Domestic, of the Reign of Henry VIII*, ed. James Gairdner and R. H. Brodie, 21 vols. (1862–1932) [hereafter *LP*], vol. XXI (ii) nos. 203, 212, 417–21.

The text of the 1542 Act (33° Henry VIII c. 8) is available in *Statutes of the Realm, printed by command of his majesty King George III* (1817), vol. III, p. 837; the general Act of Repeal of 1547 is at vol. IV, pp. 18–22.

Accounts of Lord Henry's public career and his tenure as fifth earl of Westmorland can be found in James E. Doyle, *The Official Baronage of England* (1886), vol. III, pp. 634–5, or in the *Oxford Dictionary of National Biography*. See also the account of the Neville family's career in Mervyn James, *Family, Lineage and Civil Society: A Study of Society, Politics and Mentality in the Durham Region, 1500–1640* (1974). The account of the plot of 1549 is in W. K. Jordan (ed.), *The Chronicle and Political Papers of King Edward VI* (1966), sub. 11 October 1552.

Related documents on the case, on Lord Henry, and on Ninian Menville can be found in *LP* vols. XII (i) no. 978, XII (ii) no. 191.3, XVIII (i) no. 464, XIX (ii) no. 334, XX (ii) no. 633, XX (ii) Appendix 2, XXI (i) no. 1235; Charles Wriothesley, *A Chronicle of England during the Reigns of the Tudors*, ed. W. D. Hamilton, vol. I (Camden Society new series XI, 1875), p. 50; C. S. Knighton (ed.), *Calendar of State Papers of the Reign of Edward VI 1547–1553* (1992), nos. 44, 466, 717; C. S. Knighton (ed.), *Calendar of State Papers*

Domestic Series: Mary I 1553–1558 (1998), nos. 423, 794; *Acts of the Privy Council of England*, ed. John R. Dasent (1890–), vol. II, pp. 458–9, 487, vol. III, pp. 224–6, 448–9, 473–98, vol. IV, pp. 17, 49–50, 212–20, 330, 351, 417; *Calendar of State Papers Relating to Scotland and Mary, Queen of Scots, 1547–1563*, ed. Joseph Bain (1898), nos. 416, 533, 658; *Calendar of State Papers, Foreign Series, of the Reign of Elizabeth, 1559–60*, ed. Joseph Stevenson (1865), nos. 81, 336; *Correspondence of Matthew Parker, D.D., Archbishop of Canterbury*, ed. John Bruce (1853), p. 105; Lambeth Palace Library, MS 3205 fo. 18 (*LP* vol. XX (i) no. 575). The proverb about Jewish magicians is in Edward Worsop, *A Discoverie of sundrie errours and faults daily committed by Lande-meaters* (1582), sig. F4v.

CHAPTER 2

The account given of the Wisdoms' medical career is constructed from the Annals of the Royal College of Physicians (see vol. I, fos. 4r, 6r, 31r; vol. II, fos. 15r–v, 18r, 20r, 22v–23v; cf. transcript held at the Royal College); NA, C 82/797/47 (cf. *LP* XVII, no. 443.2); NA, E 159/320 Trinity rot. 13, 16; William Munk, *The Roll of the Royal College of Physicians of London*, 2nd edn, 4 vols (1878); G. A. T. Allen (ed.), *Christ's Hospital Admissions, vol. I: 1554–99* (1937), p. 163; Sidney Young (ed.), *The Annals of the Barber-Surgeons of London* (1890), p. 524. The relevant legislation is at *Statutes of the Realm*, III, pp. 31–2, 906. The Royal College of Physicians' lawsuit against unlicensed surgeons in 1541, and its consequences, are carefully narrated in Raymond Stanley Roberts, 'The London Apothecaries and Medical Practice in Tudor and Stuart England' (University of London PhD thesis, 1964), pp. 42–51.

On the whole subject of the medical profession's status and attempts at self-regulation, the work of Margaret Pelling is indispensable: see especially her 'Appearance and Reality: Barber-Surgeons, the Body and Disease', in A. L. Beier and Roger Finlay (eds), *London 1500–1700: The Making of the Metropolis* (1986), pp. 82–112, and her *Medical Conflicts in Early Modern London* (2003). On the pox, see Jon Arrizabagala, John Henderson, and Roger

French, *The Great Pox: The French Disease in Renaissance Europe* (1997), and Andrew Cunningham and Ole Peter Grell, *The Four Horsemen of the Apocalypse: Religion, War, Famine and Death in Reformation Europe* (2000).

For Bishop Earle's satirical view of physicians and surgeons, see John Earle, *The Autograph Manuscript of* Microcosmographie (1966), pp. 12–17, 113–15. For Bishop Latimer's comments, see George Elwes Corrie (ed.), *Sermons by Hugh Latimer* (1844), pp. 539–41; Sancroft's lugubrious verdict is quoted in Patrick Collinson, 'William Sancroft', in his *From Cranmer to Sancroft* (2006), p. 178. For the medical establishment's fightback after the Quacks' Charter, see John Caius, *A boke or counseill against the disease commonly called the sweate or sweatynge sicknesse* (1552), fos. 27v–28v; Thomas Gale (ed.), *Certaine Workes of Galens, called Methodus Medendi, with a briefe Declaration of the worthie Art of Medicine* (1586), fos. 32r–33r; and John Securis, *A detection and querimonie of the daily enormities and abuses committed in physick* (1566), sigs. B2r–3r, C3v.

John and Gregory Wisdom's wills are both held at the Guildhall Library in the City of London—see MS 9171/15 fo. 99r and 9051/5 fos. 139v–141r, respectively. The 'book called the Dannel' is in the British Library, Sloane MS 3853, fo. 176 ff.; I am grateful to Frank Klaasen for drawing my attention to this book, and to Robert Mathieson for identifying Gordonio as the author of John Wisdom's other book. On Gordonio, see Luke E. Demaitre, *Doctor Bernard de Gordon: Professor and Practitioner* (1980), esp. pp. 21–8, 51–6. For further detail on the Wisdom family tree, see the wills of Gregory's elder brother John Wisdom (d. 1574), and of John's wife Joan (d. 1576–7), at NA, PCC Prob. 11/56 fos. 320r–321r and PCC Prob. 11/59 fos. 66r–67v, respectively; a lawsuit between John the younger and his son-in-law Lawrence Broadbent, at NA, C 31/10/71; and see Chapter 5. The lease of Painters' Hall to the Wisdoms and others is in the Guildhall Library, MS 5670/16. There is further background on the family's property in *LP* XVIII (i) no. 346.66, XIX (ii) no. 527.3, and in R. G. Lang (ed.), *Two Tudor Subsidy Assessment Rolls for the City of London* (London

Record Society, 1993), pp. 10, 16 (where 'George' is presumably a scribal error for 'Gregory'), 141. Gregory's arrest in 1553 is recorded in John R. Dasent (ed.), *Acts of the Privy Council of England*, vol. IV (1892), pp. 274–5. For Davy Cromwell's astronomy book, see Norman Moore, *The History of St. Bartholomew's Hospital*, 2 vols. (1918), vol. II, p. 274.

The lawsuits against Gregory Wisdom from the 1540s are both preserved in the National Archives: the Bendyshe case is C1/1085/73 and the Wentworth case is REQ 2/9/82.

CHAPTER 3

Gilbert Walker's book (*A manifest detection of the moste vyle and detestable vse of Diceplay*) is undated, and the surviving edition probably dates from 1555, but there was apparently an earlier edition, since one section of the text refers to the 1544 siege of Boulogne as being fresh and exciting news (see sig. A6v). It, and much of the rest of the rogue literature of the sixteenth and early seventeenth century, are included in an invaluable anthology edited by A. V. Judges: *The Elizabethan Underworld* (1930). Other pamphlets drawn on here are *The seuerall notorious and levvd cousnages of Iohn West, and Alice West* (1613) and *The Brideling, Sadling and Ryding, of a rich Churle in Hampshire, by the subtill practise of one Iudeth Philips* (1595).

The broad subject of crime and disorder in Tudor England, and in London in particular, has been well served by recent historians. Essential reading includes James Sharpe, *Crime in Early Modern England, 1550–1750* (1999, cf. 1st edn 1984); A. L. Beier, *Masterless Men: The Vagrancy Problem in England, 1560–1640* (1985); and Ian Archer, *The Pursuit of Stability: Social Relations in Elizabethan London* (1991). Most of this work, however, concentrates on the great mass of 'ordinary' criminality, not on the rarefied worlds of organized crime or complex fraud. John L. McMullan, *The Canting Crew: London's Criminal Underworld 1550–1700* (1984) pays more attention to that subject, but is perhaps too credulous of the rogue literature. That literature's boundaries between fact and fiction are explored in Paul Griffiths, 'Overlapping Circles: Imagining Criminal Communities in London, 1545–1645', in *Communities in Early Modern England*, ed. Alexandra Shepard and Phil Withington (2002).

For contemporary denunciations of gambling, see—amongst many others—*The Works of Roger Hutchinson*, ed. John Bruce (1842), p. 7; John Northbrooke, 'A Treatise against Dicing, Dancing, Plays and Interludes', in *Early Treatises on the Stage* (Shakespeare Society, vol. 15, 1843), pp. 104–44; Thomas Elyot, *The boke named the Gouernour, deuised by s Thomas Elyot knight* (1531), fos. 95v–97v; and especially John Harington, 'A treatise on Playe', in his *Nugae Antiquae*, ed. Henry Harington, 3 vols. (1779), vol. II, pp. 154–208.

The best survey of London prostitution is Paul Griffiths, 'The Structure of Prostitution in Elizabethan London', *Continuity and Change*, 8 (1993). See also Wallace Shugg, 'Prostitution in Shakespeare's London', in *Shakespeare Studies*, 10 (1977), and Ruth Mazo Karras, *Common Women: Prostitution and Sexuality in Medieval England* (1996). On the sexual double standard, see the classic article by Keith Thomas, 'The Double Standard', *Journal of the History of Ideas*, 20 (1959).

Pilkington's comments on St Paul's are found in James Pilkington, *The burnynge of Paules church in London in the yeare of oure Lord 1561* (1563), sig. G5v. The account of Wotton's school for pickpockets is printed in R. H. Tawney and Eileen Power (eds), *Tudor Economic Documents*, 3 vols. (1924), vol. III, pp. 337–9. Hall's attack on the quacks of Maidstone is in his 'An Historiall Expostulation', ed. T. J. Pettigrew, in *Early English Poetry, Ballads, and Popular Literature of the Middle Ages* (Percy Society, vol. XI, 1844), pp. 6–11. The case of Cesare Adelmari is described in Alwyn A. Ruddock, 'The Earliest Records of the High Court of Admiralty (1515–1588)', in *Bulletin of the Institute of Historical Research*, 22 (1949), 145. For Latimer's views on prostitution, see his *Sermons*, p. 196. In Jonson's *The Alchemist*, see especially I.ii.16–30, 77–82, 143–7; II.v.87–90. The modern 'cheater' cited is the proprietor of Cardshark Online (http://cardshark.us/home.html).

For examples of rituals to summon fairies, see two manuscripts in the Folger Shakespeare Library, Washington: V.b.26 and X.d.234. Other references cited are *LP* XXI (ii) 199.iii; Shakespeare's *Henry IV, Part I*, I.ii, and his *Julius Caesar*, II.i.285–6; *Statutes of the Realm*, III, pp. 837–41; IV, p. 488; Henry Parker, *Dives and Pauper* (1493), sig. b7r–v; William H. Hale, *A Series of Precedents and Proceedings in Criminal Causes* (1847), pp. 32–3.

CHAPTER 4

All writing on magic in England revolves around one monumental book: Keith Thomas, *Religion and the Decline of Magic* (1971), a vast and brilliant survey which has aged exceptionally well, and is still immensely readable. (Amongst other things, Thomas briefly noted Wisdom's case—pp. 275, 280—although without identifying him.) Many themes touched on briefly in this chapter are explored in much more depth there.

On Renaissance magic from Ficino to Agrippa, see above all Frances Yates' classic, *Giordano Bruno and the Hermetic Tradition* (1964); also Christopher I. Lehrich, *The Language of Demons and Angels: Cornelius Agrippa's Occult Philosophy* (2003). The musical dimension of Renaissance magic is delightfully explored in Jamie James, *The Music of the Spheres: Music, Science and the Natural Order of the Universe* (1995). Alchemy in general is surveyed in F. Sherwood Taylor, *The Alchemists: Founders of Modern Chemistry* (1951), and the case of Georg Honauer in Tara E. Nummedal, 'The Problem of Fraud in Early Modern Alchemy', in Mark Crane, Richard Raiswell, and Margaret Reeves (eds), *Shell Games: Studies in Scams, Frauds and Deceits (1300–1650)* (2004). The best guide to astrology in general is Jim Tester, *A History of Western Astrology* (1987); the almanac trade is authoritatively described in Bernard Capp, *Astrology and the Popular Press: English Almanacs, 1500–1800* (1979). On Girolamo Cardano, see Anthony Grafton, *Cardano's Cosmos* (1999).

The almanacs and astrological textbooks cited are Andrew Boorde, *The pryncyples of Astronomye the whiche diligently perscrutyd is in maner a pronosticacyon to the worldes end compylyd by Andrew Boord of phisick Doctor* (1547?); Anthony Askham, *A litell treatyse of astrouomy, very necessary for Physyke and Surgerye* (1550); Anthony Askham, *An almanacke and prognostication for the yere of our Lorde God MDLV* (1555); John Securis, *An almanacke and prognostication for the yere 1562* (1562).

On ritual magic and conjuring, see the dated but still valuable E. M. Butler, *Ritual Magic* (1949), and Claire Fanger (ed.), *Conjuring Spirits: Texts and Traditions of Medieval Ritual Magic* (1998). The most easily accessible text is S. L. M. Mathers (ed.), *The Key of Solomon the King (Clavicula Salomonis)* (1972). The account of the conjurers of Edmonton and the case of John Buckley are amongst several incidents in this chapter narrated in W. H. Hart, 'Observations on Some Documents Relating to Magic in the Reign of Queen Elizabeth', *Archaeologia*, 40 (1866), 389–97. The 1549 cases of William Wycherley and of Alen are found in John G. Nichols (ed.), *Narratives of the Days of the Reformation* (Camden Society, old series vol. 77, 1859), pp. 172–5, 326–35. The 'Dannel' is British Library, Sloane MS 3853 fo. 176 ff.

Other sources cited include F. H. Mares' comment from his edition of *The Alchemist* (1971), p. xxxv. For John Hooper's views on magic, see his *Early Writings*, ed. Samuel Carr (1843), pp. 326–7. For Henry VIII's fondness for astrology and physiognomy, see *Miscellaneous Writings and Letters of Thomas Cranmer* (1846). The case of the 'natural' magician who experimented on his daughter is found in the Bodleian Library, Oxford, MS Ashmolean 421, fos. 231–2. For John Earle's comment on alchemy, see *The Autograph Manuscript of* Microcosmographie (1966), p. 16. Elizabeth I's interest in alchemy is documented in Mary Anne Everett Green (ed.), *Calendar of State Papers, Domestic Series, of the Reign of Elizabeth, 1591–94* (1867), nos. 422, 435. For John Hall's view of astrology, see John Hall, 'An Historiall Expostulation', ed. T. J. Pettigrew, in *Early English Poetry, Ballads, and Popular Literature of the Middle Ages* (Percy Society vol. XI, 1844), pp. 37–8. Calvin's view of astrology is given in his *An admonicion against astrology iudiciall* (1561). Jean de Monluc's mathematical researches are described in James

Melville of Halhill, *Memoirs of his own life*, ed. T. Thomson (1827).
For the astrologers who foretold that Elizabeth I would be a boy,
see *LP* VI, no. 1112. For other denunciations of magic, see William
Fulke, *Antiprognosticon that is to saye, an inuectiue agaynst the vayne
and vnprofitable predictions of the astrologians as Nostrodame* (1560);
Francis Cox, *A short treatise declaringe the detestable wickednesse, of
magicall sciences* (1561); Laurence Humphrey, *The nobles, or of nobilitye* (1563, cf. Latin edn, 1560); and Anthony Gilby, *A Commentarye
vpon the Prophet Mycha* (1551), sigs K4r-5v.

The report of the earl of Westmorland's interest in Nostradamus is in NA, SP 12/23, fo. 31r. The story of the friends finding the mathematical notebook is in Edward Worsop, *A Discouerie
of sundrie errours and faults daily committed by Lande-meaters* (1582),
sig. C1r. William Blomefield's exploits are recounted in NA, SP
1/222, fo. 132r (*LP* XXI (i) no. 1360). The tale of Charlemagne and
the magic ring was told by William Tyndale, in his *Expositions and
Notes on Sundry Portions of the Holy Scriptures*, ed. Henry Walter
(1849), p. 265. The reference to the conjurer Dr Elkes is in NA,
SP 186/92, no. 92; the case of Adam Squier is described in C. H.
Herford, Percy Simpson, and Evelyn Simpson, *Ben Jonson: vol. X*
(1950), pp. 62-3. John Curson and the treasure of Kettering are
described in Edward Peacock, 'Extracts from Lincoln Episcopal
Visitations in the 15th, 16th and 17th Centuries', *Archaeologia*, 48,
part 2 (1885), p. 255; the Yorkshire diviner of 1467 in James Raine,
'Divination in the Fifteenth Century by Aid of a Magical Crystal',
in *The Archaeological Journal*, 13 (1856), 372-4. The case of the wax
child from 1538 is detailed in *LP* XIII (i) no. 41, that of Elizabeth
Celsay in *LP* XVIII (ii) no. 546, p. 300, and that of Mabel Brigge
in *LP* XIII (i) nos. 487, 705. William Neville's plots are described in
G. R. Elton, *Policy and Police: The Enforcement of the Reformation
in the Age of Thomas Cromwell* (1972), pp. 50-6.

CHAPTER 5

On Robert Wisdom's career, see the *Oxford Dictionary of National
Biography*. His denunciation of ghosts is in the British Library,

Harleian MS 425, fo. 6v; on his uncle John's support for him, see Emmanuel College, Cambridge, MS 261, fos. 92v–93r, and Guildhall Library, London, MS 9531/12, fos. 45r–v. The will of John Wisdom senior is also in the Guildhall Library, MS 9171/15, fo. 99r; that of John Wisdom junior in NA, PCC Prob. 11/56, fos. 320r–321r, and that of Joan Wisdom in NA, PCC Prob 11/59, fos. 66r–67v. On Simon Wisdom, see John Foxe, *Actes and monuments of matters most speciall in the church* (1583), p. 985; NA, E334/2, fo. 152r, E334/3, fos. 13v, 26r.

Protestant denunciations of magic are too common to list, but noteworthy examples include John Hooper's attack on astrology, found in his *Early Writings* (1843), pp. 326–33. Hutchinson's subtler discussion is in *The Works of Roger Hutchinson*, ed. John Bruce (1842), pp. 69–89; Calvin's treatise is *An admonicion against Astrology Iudiciall and other curiosities, that raigne now in the world*, trans. George Gylby (1561). William Fulke, *Antiprognosticon, that is to saye, an inuectiue agaynst the vayne and vnprofitable predictions of the astrologians* (1560) is a blunt denial that astrology was possible. The spoof almanac quoted is the anonymous *A mery pronosticacion for the yere a thousande fyue hundreth fortye and foure* (1544).

For Bale's association of Catholicism with magic, see, amongst many other examples in his voluminous and often disgustingly scatalogical works, his *The lattre examinacyon of Anne Askewe* (1547), fo. 60r, and Peter Happé (ed.), *The Complete Plays of John Bale*, vol. 2 (1986), pp. 79–82. For parallel allegations see, again amongst many examples, James Calfhill, *An answer to John Martiall's Treatise of the Cross*, ed. Richard Gibbings (1846), pp. 14–17; and the anonymous *Here begynneth a boke, called the faull of the romyshe churche* (1547?), sig. B4v. On the 'miraculous' rood of Boxley, see Peter Marshall, 'The Rood of Boxley, the Blood of Hailes and the Defence of the Henrician Church', in *Journal of Ecclesiastical History*, 46 (1995), 689–96. On the attempt to recast Catholic popes and saints as sorcerers, see Helen Parish, *Monks, Miracles and Magic: Reformation Representations of the Medieval Church* (2005). For Catholic dislike of magic, see Walter Frere and William Kennedy, *Visitation Articles and Injunctions of the Period of the Reformation* (Alcuin Club Collections 14–16, 1910), vol. II, pp. 353, 388, 425 (and cf. p. 111). Edmund Bonner's fulmination against magic is taken from his *A profitable and necessarye doctrine* (1555), sig. Hh2r–v, and Richard Whitford's from *A werke for housholders, or for them that haue the gydyng or gouernaunce of ony company* (1530), sig. C2r–v.

For Protestants who denied the legitimacy of magic but accepted its reality, see William Tyndale, *Doctrinal Treatises and Introductions to Different Portions of the Holy Scriptures* (1848), p. 413; Anthony Gilby, *A Commentarye vpon the Prophet Mycha* (1551), sig. K6v; John Jewel, *The Works of John Jewel, Bishop of Salisbury* (1847), pp. 1027–8; *The Works of Roger Hutchinson*, ed. John Bruce (1842), p. 142; John Hall, 'An Historiall Expostulation', in *Early English Poetry, Ballads, and Popular Literature of the Middle Ages* (Percy Society vol. XI, 1844), pp. 29–30, and cf. pp. 6–7, 9, 37–8. For the legitimacy of astrology, see Laurence Humphrey, *The nobles, or of nobilitye* (1563), sig. y7r; Edward Worsop, *A Discoverie of sundrie errours and faults daily committed by Lande-meaters* (1582), sigs. E4r– G1v; and Calvin's *Admonicion*. Coverdale's Protestantized almanac is *A faythfull and true pronostication vpon the yere. M.CCCCC.xlviii.* (1547; cf. 1st edn, 1535). On Protestant almanacs more generally, see Bernard Capp, *Astrology and the Popular Press: English Almanacs, 1500–1800* (1979). For John Borthwick's astrological enterprises, see *LP* XX (i) no. 1240. For Bomelius, see the *Oxford Dictionary of National Biography*. James Melville of Halhill's tale of the palmister Taggot is in his *Memoirs of his own life*, ed. T. Thomson (1827), pp. 19–20.

Faustian pacts, and the case of the student from Tübingen, are discussed sensibly in E. M. Butler, *Ritual Magic* (1949), pp. 204– 15. William Byg's case is described in James Raine, 'Divination in the Fifteenth Century by Aid of a Magical Crystal' in *The Archaeological Journal*, 13 (1856), 372–4. The account of the astrologer–physician who feared idolatry is in the Bodleian Library, Ashmolean MS 421, fos. 231–2. The Elizabethan grimoire cited is Folger Shakespeare Library MS V.b.26. G. K. Chesterton's famous opinion was most succinctly expressed as 'The first effect of not believing in God is to believe in anything'—not by Chesterton himself, but by his early biographer Émile Cammaerts, in *The Laughing Prophet* (1937). For William Cunningham's excitement at the intellectual possibilities of the Renaissance, see his *The cosmographical glasse, conteinyng the pleasant principles of cosmographie, geographie, hydrographie, or nauigation* (1559), sig. A5r–v, pp. 6–10, 37, 186–90, and his *Nevve almanacke and prognostication, collected for [the] yere of our Lord, M. D. Lviii* (1558), sig. A2v.

On Lord Henry's religiosity, see Alec Ryrie, *The Gospel and Henry VIII* (2003), pp. 211–12. For the 1556 plotters' view of him, see C. S. Knighton (ed.), *Calendar of State Papers Domestic Series: Mary I 1553–1558* (1998), no. 423. The letter of Lord Henry's quoted is NA, SP 1/226, fo. 125v (*LP* XXI (ii) no. 419).

Photographic Acknowledgements

Cabinet des Estampes, Bibliothèque nationale de France, Paris: **5**; Bodleian Library, University of Oxford: **10** (40 G 8 (5) Art.BS.), (80 K 3 (2) Art.BS.) **7**; British Library: **12** (Sloane MS 3853 fo. 184v.), **13** (Sloane MS 3853 fo. 205v.); Mary Evans Picture Library: **4**; Floger Shakespeare Library: **14**; Guildhall Library, City of London (MS 9051/5, fos. 139v–141r.): **15**; Huntington Library, San Marino, California (RB 62881): **11**; Kimbell Art Museum, Fort Worth, Texas (AP 1987.06)/ Art Resource, New York: **8**; Musee d'Art et d'Histoire, Saint-Germain-en-Laye, France/Giraudon/The Bridgeman Art Library: **9**; Public Record Office (SP 1/226 fo. 128r.) : **1**; Alec Ryrie: **2**, **3**.

Index